TIBETAN GRAMMAR

H. A. JÄSCHKE

•

TIBETAN GRAMMAR

•

Supplement of Readings with Vocabulary by

JOHN L. MISH

Chief, Oriental Division, New York Public Library

•

FREDERICK UNGAR PUBLISHING CO.
NEW YORK

The main body of the *GRAMMAR*
is based on the second edition
as prepared by H. Wenzel.

PUBLISHERS' NOTE

Since it is so difficult for the student to obtain any kind of material in the Tibetan language, we are issuing this new printing of Jäschke's well-known text, which has been largely unavailable for many years.

The reading matter has been expanded by the addition of a selection from *Mdzangs-blun*, third chapter, according to the Schmidt edition. To increase the value of the present text for the reader, we have added a helpful Vocabulary in which the student will find all words in the reading exercises.

Abbreviations.

act. = active.

C or CT = Central Tibet, especially the provinces of Ü and Tsaṅ.

cf. = confer, compare.

Dzl. = Dzaṅlun.

e. g. = exempli gratia, for instance.

ET = East Tibet.

fut. = future.

imp. = imperative.

inf. = infinitive.

i. o. = instead of.

Köpp. = Köppen.

Kun. = Kunawur, province under English protection.

Ld. = Ladak, province.

Mil. = Milaraspa.

neutr. = neuter verb.

perf. or pf. = perfect.

pres. = present.

s. = see.

term. = terminative case.

Thgy. = Thar - gyan, scientific treatises.

v. = vide, see.

vulg. = vulgar expression.

W or WT = Western Tibet.

Contents.

I. Phonology.

II. Etymology.
I. Article.

II. Substantive.

III. Adjective.

IV. Numerals.

Contents.

Errata.

———

Page 3, line 13 read at instead of in.

„ 4, „ 2 „ respectively.

„ 4, „ 7 „ which instead of whom.

„ 4, „ 9 „ under particular.

„ 4, „ 14 „ هَمْزَة instead of هَمُونَة.

„ 4, „ 20 „ exertion.

„ 4, „ 21 dele to.

„ 5, „ 5 dele down.

„ 7, „ 4 read succession instead of conjunction.

„ 7, „ 5 „ each instead of either.

„ 7, „ 11 „ subscribed instead of subjoined.

„ 8, „ 11 „ foot for food.

„ 8, „ 12 „ subscribed for subjoined.

„ 8, „ 16 „ homonyms.

„ 8, „ 19 „ language.

„ 8, „ 23 „ over instead of above.

„ 8, „ 24 „ consonants.

„ 9, „ 10 „ case.

„ 10, „ 4 „ judgment.

„ 11, „ 9 „ except.

„ 12, „ 21 „ it instead of is.

„ 13, „ 1 „ which serve to denote.

„ 13, „ 7 „ preceding.

„ 14, „ 6 „ exclamation.

„ 20, „ 3 „ indiscriminately.

„ 20, „ 5 „ superseded.

„ 20, „ 19 „ But.

„ 21, „ 5 „ adds.

page 23, line 1 read motion.
„ 26, „ 13 „ terminations.
„ 26, „ 24 „ precedes.
„ 26, „ 27 „ higher than.
„ 33, „ 6 „ to denote.
„ 34, „ 14 „ letter-writing.
„ 36, „ 1 „ The terms most &c.
„ 36, „ 16 „ high person speaking of himself.
„ 38, „ 11 „ ghaṅ.
„ 39, „ 14 „ you may.
„ 40, „ 7 „ verbs.
„ 40, „ 21 „ an Accusative.
„ 40, „ 25 „ neutre.
„ 41, „ 10 „ form instead of shape.
„ 41, „ 11 „ forms instead of shapes.
„ 41, „ 22 „ the Perfect prefers.
„ 42, „ 1 „ Perfect.
„ 42, „ 16 „ recognises instead of acknowledges.
„ 43, „ 20 „ idea instead of notion.
„ 45, „ 14 „ with the exception.
„ 46, „ 6 „ which will always be.
„ 46, „ 10 „ to one.
„ 52, „ 15 „ it expresses.
„ 53, „ 11 „ found.
„ 53, „ 24 „ passive sense, opposed to &c.
„ 55, „ 7 „ affixes.
„ 58, „ 12 „ that it.
„ 61, „ 12 „ king's.
„ 64, „ 8 „ intended.

„ 66, „ 15 „ རབ་ཏུ ‚principally, very‘;

Part I.

Phonology.

1. The Alphabet. The Tibetan Alphabet was adapted from the *Lañča* (ལཉྩ) form of the Indian letters by *Ton-mi-sam-bho-ta* (ཐོན་མི་སམ་བྷོ་ཏ) minister of king *Sron-tsan-gam-po* (སྲོང་བཙན་སྒམ་པོ) about the year 632 (s. Köpp. II, 56). The Indian letters out of which the single Tibetan characters were formed are given in the following table in their Nāgari shape.

	surd.	aspir.	sonant.	nasal.
gutturals. .	ཀ क *ka*	ཁ ख *k̑a*	ག ग *ga*	ང ङ *ṅa*
palatals. . .	ཙ च *ča*	ཚ छ *ča*	ཛ ज *ja*	ཉ ञ *ña*
dentals. . .	ཏ त *ta*	ཐ थ *t̑a*	ད द *da*	ན न *na*
labials. . .	པ प *pa*	ཕ फ *p̑a*	བ ब *ba*	མ म *ma*
palatal si-} bilants. .}	ཙ *tsa*	ཚ *t̑sa*	ཛ *dsa*	
	ཝ व *wa*	ཞ ष *ža*	ཟ *za*	འ *ₔa*
semivowels	ཡ य *ya*	ར र *ra*	ལ ल *la*	
	ཤ ष *ša*	ས स *sa*	ཧ ह *ha*	ཨ *'a*

It is seen from this table that several signs have been added to express sounds that are unknown in Sanscrit. The sibilants ཙ་ ཚ་ ཛ་ evidently were differentiated from the palatals. But as in transcribing Sanscrit words the Tibetans substitute their sibilants for the palatals of the original (as ཙིན་ for चीन), we must suppose that the sibilisation of those consonants, common at present among the Hindus on the Southern slopes of the Himālaya (who speak *tsār* for चार, four etc.), was in general use with those Indians from whom the Tib. Alphabet was taken (cf. also the Afghan ‿ and ⁚ likewise sprung from ‿ and ‿). ཞ is differentiated from ཟ, which itself often is pronounced *v*, as shewn in the sequel; in transcribing Sanscrit, ब and व both are given, generally, by ཝ only. ཝ seems to be formed out of འ to which it is related in sound. ཤ evidently is only the inverted ཥ. ཨ corresponds with Sanscrit अ. ཿ is newly invented; for its functions see the following §§. — The letters which are peculiar to Sanscrit are expressed, in transcribing, in the following manner. *a*) The linguals, simply by inverting the signs of the dentals: thus, ཊ ट, ཋ ठ, ཌ ड, ཎ ण. *b*) The sonant aspirates, by putting ྷ under the sonants: thus, གྷ घ, ཇྷ झ, ཌྷ ढ, དྷ ध, བྷ भ.*)

---

*) A very clear exposition of the ramification of Indian alphabets by Dr. Haas is to be found in the Publications of the Palaeographical Society Oriental Series IV, pl XLIV.

2. Remarks. 1. Regarding the pronunciation of the single letters, as given above, it is to be born in mind, that surds ग ད བ are uttered without the least admixture of an aspiration, viz. as *k, t, p* are pronounced in the words *skate, stale, spear*; the aspirates ཁ ཐ ཕ forcibly, rather harder than the same in *Kate, tale, peer*; the sonants ག ད བ like *g, d, b* in *gate, dale, beer*. 2. The same difference of hardness is to be observed in ཙ ཚ ཇ or *c̀, c̆, j̀* (*c̆* occurs in *church*; *c̀*, the same without aspiration; *j̀* in *judge*) and in ཙ ཚ ཛ or *ts, t͂s, ds*. 3. ཞ is the soft modification of *s̀* or the *s* in *leisure* (French *j* in *jamais*, but more palatal). 4. ང is the English *ng* in *sing*, but occurs in Tibetan often in the commencement of a syllable. 5. ཉ *ñ* is the Hindi ञ, or the initial sound in the word *new*, which would be spelled ཉུ *ñu*. 6. In the dialects of Eastern or Chinese-Tibet, however, the soft consonants ག ད བ ཇ ཛ, when occurring as initials, are pronounced with an aspiration, similar to the Hindi घ, ध, भ, झ, or indeed so that they often scarcely differ from the common English *k, t, p, ch*; also ཞ and ཟ are more difficult to distinguish from ཤ and ས than in the Western provinces (Exceptions s. §§ 7. 8).

3. Vowels. 1. Since every consonant sign implies, like its Sanscrit prototype, a following *a*, unless some other vowel sign is attached to it, no particular sign is wanted to denote this vowel, except in some cases specified in the following §§. The special vowel signs are ◠, ◠, ◡, ◡, pronounced respectivily as *e, i, o, u* are in German, Italian and most other European languages, viz. ◠ like *ay* in *say*, or *e* in *ten*; ◠ like *i* in *machine, tin*; ◡ like *o* in *so, on*; ◡ like *u* in *rule, pull*. It ought to be specially remarked that all vowels, including *e* and *o* (unlike the Sanscrit vowels from whom they have taken their signs) are short, since no long vowels at all occur in the Tibetan language, except particular circumstances, mentioned below (s. § 9. 5, 6). ② When vowels are initial, ཨ is used as their base, as is ا in Urdu, e. g. ཨ་མ *ama*, ,mother'. 3. འ is originally different from ཨ, as the latter denotes the opening of the previously closed throat for pronouncing a vowel with that slight explosive sound which the Arabs mean by ا (همزة), as the *a* in the words: the *lily, an* endogen, which would be in Tibetan characters ལི་ལི་ཨན; འ on the contrary is the mere vowel *without* that audible opening of the throat (as Arabic ا without ء), as in *Lilian*, ལི་ལི་འན In Eastern Tibet this difference is strictly observed; and if the vowel is *o* or *u* the intentional exercion for avoiding the sound of ཨ makes it resemble to *wo* and *wu*: འོ་མ ,the milk', almost like *wo-ma*, འུག་པ ,the owl' = *wug-pa*. In western Tibet this has been obliterated, and འ is there spoken just like ཨ

4. Syllables. The Tibetan language is monosyllabic, that is to say all its words consist of one syllable only, which indeed may be variously composed, though the componen*t* parts cannot, in every case, be recognised in their individuality. The mark for the end of such a syllable is a dot, called ཚེག་ *tseg*, put at the right side of the upper part of the closing letter, such as ཀ་ the syllable *ka*. This *tseg* must invariably be put down at the end of *each* written syllable, except before a *šad* (§ 10), in which case only ང་ *ṅa* retains its *tseg*. If therefore such a dot is found after two or more consonants, this will indicate that all of them, some way or other, fòrm *one* syllable with only *one* vowel in it: ཀ་ར་ *ka-ra*, ཀར་ *kar* (cf. §§ 5. 8).

5. Final consonants. 1. Only the following ten: ག་ ང་ ད་ ན་ བ་ མ་ འ་ ར་ ལ་ ས་ (and the four with affixed ས་, v. 5) occur at the end of a syllable. 2. It must be observed, that ག་ ད་ བ་ as finals are never pronounced like the English *g, d, b* in *leg, bad, cab*, but are transformed differently in the different provinces. In Ladak they sound like *k, t, p* e. g. སོག་ = *sock*, གོད་ = *got*, ཐོབ་ = *top*. 3. In all Central Tibet, moreover, final ད་ and ན་, sometimes even ལ་, modify the sound of a preceeding vowel: *a* to *ä* (similar to the English *a* in *hare, man*), *o* into *ǫ* (French *eu* in *jeu*), *u* into *ü* (French *u* in *mur*). In most of the other provinces ག་ and ད་ are uttered so indistinctly as to be scarcely audible, so that སོག་, གོད་ become *sŏ', gŏ'*. In Tsang even final ལ་ is scarcely perceptible, and final ག་, particularly after *o*, is almost dissolved into a vowel sound = a: སོལ་བ་ *so-wa*,

དཀོན་མཆོག་ *kon-choa.**)   4. Final ས་ is sounded as *s* only
in Northern Ladak; elsewhere it changes into *i* or
dissappears entirely, prolonging, or even modifying at the
same time the preceding vowel. Thus the following words:
ནས་ ‚barley‘, ཤེས་ ‚know‘, རིས་ ‚figure‘, ཆོས་ ‚religion‘, ལུས་
‚body‘, are pronounced in Northern Ladak: *năs, šĕs, ris,*
čos, lŭs; in Lahoul: *nai, shei, rī, čō, lū;* in Lhasa, and
consequently by everyone who wishes to speak elegantly:
nạ̄, šē, rī, čọ̈, lụ̄.   5. In some words final ས་ occurs as
a second closing letter (affix), after ག་ ང་ བ་ མ་, as in

ནགས་ ‚forest‘, གངས་ ‚glacier-ice‘, ཐབས་ ‚means‘, རམས་
‚indigo‘; these are pronounced in N. Ladak: *nacks, gaṅs, ťaps,*
rams, elsewhere *nack* (in Ü: *nā*), *gaṅ* (ET *ghang*), *ťap, ram.*
6. ན་ before པ་ and མ་ is especially in ET very often pronounced *m,* e.g. ཉན་པ་ *ñäm-pa,* ཉོན་པ་ *ñöm-pa,* སྙེམ་པ་ *ñem-pa.*

6. Dipthongs.   1. They occur in Tibetan writing only
where one of the vowels *i, o, u* have to be added to a word
ending with an other vowel (s. §§ 15. 1; 33. 1; 45. 2). These
additional vowels are then always written འི་, འོ་, འུ་,
never ཨི་ etc. (cf. § 3. 3); and the combinations *ai, oi, ui*
(as in བགའི་, མགོའི་, བུའི་) are pronounced very much
like *ạ̈, ọ̈, ụ̈,* so that the syllables ནའི་, ཤའི་, རིའི་, ཆོའི་,

---

**) This is the form in which the word, chosen by the missionaries
to express the Christian „God“ (cf. dict.), has found its way into
several popular works.*

སྟུའི་ can only in some vulgar dialects be distinguished from those mentioned in § 5. 4. 2. The others *ao, eo, io, oo, uo, au, eu, iu* (བཀའ་, སྐྱེའི་, བགྱིའི་, འགྲོའི་, འདུའི་, གཱུ་, བྱེའི་, ཁྱིའི་) are pronounced in rapid conjunction, but either vowel is distinctly audible. In prosody they are generally regarded as one syllable, but if the verse should require it they may be counted as two.

7. Compound consonants. 1. They are expressed in writing by putting one below the other, in which case several change their original figure.

Subjoined consonants. 2. The letter *y* subjoined to another is represented by the figure ྱ, and occurs in connection with the three gutturals and labials, and with *m*, thus ཀྱ་ ཁྱ་ གྱ་ པྱ་ ཕྱ་ བྱ་ མྱ་. The former three have preserved, in most cases, their original pronunciation *kya, k̕ya, gya* (the latter in ET: *ghya* s. § 2. 6). In the Mongol pronunciation of Tibetan words, however, they have been corrupted into *č, č̕, ĵ* respectively, a well known instance of which is the common pronunciation *Kanĵur* i. o. *kangyur*, or eleg. *ka-gyur* (བཀའ་འགྱུར་). པྱ་, ཕྱ་, བྱ་ are almost everywhere spoken without any difference from ཙ, ཚ, ཛ (except in the Western dialect before *e* and *i*, where the *y* is dropped and པ་, ཕ་, བ་ alone are pronounced). མྱ་ is spoken *ny* = ཉ. 3. *r* occurs at the foot of the gutturals, dentals, labials, of ད, མ, ས, and ཧ, in the shape of ྲ. In some parts of the country, as in Purig, these combinations are pronounced literally, like *kra, khra* etc., but by far the most general custom is to sound them like the Indian cerebrals, viz. ཀྲ, ཏྲ, ཏྲ indiscriminately = ट *ṭ*; ཁྲ, ཐྲ, ཐྲ = ठ *ṭh*; གྲ, དྲ. དྲ = ड *ḍ* (in CT: *ḍh*); only in the case of བྲ the literal pronunciation *br* is not uncommon. In རྐ and རྨ both letters are distinctly heard; ཧྲ sounds like *shr* in *shrub*, and so does སྲ generally. In Ü this *r* is dropped nearly in all cases: thus, སྤ *p̍a*, སྲ *sa* etc.   4. Six letters are often found with an ལ beneath: ཀླ གླ བླ རླ སླ ཟླ; in these the ལ alone is pronounced, except in ཟླ, which sounds *da*.   5. The figure ◁, sometimes found at the food of a letter is used in Sanscrit words to express the subjoined ཝ, as in སྭ་ཧཱ་ (cf. § 9. 6) for स्वाहा; and is now pronounced by Tibetans = *ō*: *sōhā*; in words originally Tibetan it now exists merely as an orthographical mark, to distinguish homonymes in writing, as ཙ *tsa* ,hot' and ཚ *tsa* ,salt'; but, as it is spoken, in some words at least, in Balti (e. g. རྩྭ་ *rtswa* ,grass', it must be supposed that, in the primitive form of the lauguage, it was generally heard. — *Note.* Of such compounds, indeed, as ལྭ ,lot' it is difficult to understand, how they can have been pronounced literally, if the *v* was not, perhaps, pronounced before the *y*.

S u p e r a d d e d c o n s o n a n t s. 6. *r* above another consonant is written ⌐, and 11 contonants have this sign: རྐ རྒ རྔ རྗ རྙ རྟ རྡ རྣ རྩ རྫ, above ཇ it preserves its full shape, as better adapted to the form of that letter: thus, ཀྲ. In speaking it is seldom heard except provincially, and in some instances in compound words after a vowel thus, ཨུརྒྱན་ *Urgyán*, *Urgyén*, ancient name of the country of Lahore; རྡོ་རྗེ་ *dórje* ‚*vajra*‘. Ladakees often pronounce it =*s*: རྟ་ *sta* ‚horse‘ elsewhere *ta*. 7. Similar is the usage in those with a superadded ལ (namely: the surds and sonants of the first four classes, the guttural nasal, and ཧ), which latter is often softly heard in WT, but entirely dropped elsewhere, except in the ease of ལྷ, which is spoken = ལ in WT, but with a distinct aspiration = *hla* or *lha* in ET. 8. ས is superadded to the gutturals, dentals and labials with exception of the aspiratae, then ཙ and ཛ. It is, in many cases, distinctly pronounced in Ladak, but dropped elsewhere*). 9. ག་ ད་ བ་ ཇ་ ཛ་ with any superadded letter lose the aspiration mentioned in § 2. 6 and sound = *g*, *d*, *b*, *j*, *ds*. 10. ཇ་ ཟ་ ཛ་ often lose even the inherent *t*-sound in pronunciation and are spoken like *j*, *s*, *z*.

    *) This will be indicated in the following examples by including the *s* in parentheses, as *(s)kom*.

Examples.

ཀྱིར་ཀྱིར་ *kyir-kyir*, round, circular.

ཁྱི་ *kyi*, dog.

གྱེན་ལ་ *gyen-la*, upwards.

ཕྱུགས་ *čug(s)*, Ü: *čū*, cattle.

ཀྱུ་ *kyu*, hook.

ཁྱོད་ *kyod*, C: *kyö’*, you.

ཕྱུག་པོ་ *čug-po*, rich.

ཕྱེད་ W: *p̓ed*, C: *čě’*, half.

བུ་མོ་ W: *já-mo*, C: *ǰa-mo*, hen.

བྱེ་མ་ W: *bé-ma*, C: *ǰe-ma*, sand.

ཉ་ངན་ W: *ña-ṅán*, C: -*ṅän*, misery.

ཉུར་དུ་ *ñur-du*, quickly.

གྲམ་ *ṭam*, cabbage.

ཁྲལ་ *ṭal*, tax.

ཁྲིམས་ *ṭim(s)*, judgement.

གྲི་ W: *ḍi*, *ḍi* (Pur: *gri*), knife.

གྲང་མོ་ W: *daṅ-mo*, C: *ḍ°*- cold.

དྲང་པོ་ W: *ḍaṅ-po*, C: *ḍ°*, straight.

ཕྲུག་གུ་ *ṭug-gu*, child.

བྲག་ *ḍag*, *ḍag* (*brag*), rock.

སྲན་མ་ *śran-ma*, *srän-ma*, pea.

རྲུལ་པོ་ *śrul-po*, ragged.

གླ་ *la*, wages.

བླ་མ་ *lá-ma*, priest.

རླུང་(པོ་) *luṅ(-po)*, wind.

སླ་མོ་ *lá-mo*, easy.

ཟླ་བ་ *da-wa* (s. § 11 note), moon.

ཀང་པ་ *kaṅ-pa*, foot.

རྣོན་པོ་ *nón-po*, C: *nom-po*, sharp.

རྫུན་ W: *zun*, C: *dsun*, lie, untruth.

ལྗང་ཁུ་ *jaṅ-ku* (Ld. *lj°*), green.

ལྟད་མོ་ *tad-mo* (Ld. *lt°*), C: *tä-mo*, spectacle.

སྐོམ་ *(s)kom*, thirst.

སྐྲ་ W: *śra**), C: *ṭa*, hair.

སྒོ་ *(s)go*, door.

སྒྲ་ *ḍa* (vulg: *ra*), sound, voice.

སྒྱུར་བ་ *(s)gyúr-wa*, to alter, turn.

སྤུ་ *(s)pu*, small hair.

སྦྱིན་ W: *(s)pin*, C: *čin*, glue.

སྤྱོད་པ་ W: *(s)čod-pa*, C: *čö-pa*, to behave.

སྤྲེའུ་ *ṭe-u*, Ld: *śre-u*, monkey.

སྦྲུལ་ W: *(sb)rul*, C: *ḍul*, snake.

སྨན་ W: *(s)man*, C: *män*, medicine.

སྨྱོན་པ་ W: *ñon-pa*, C: *ñon-pa*, mad.

---

*) The concurrence of superadded ར་ with a consonant already

8. Prefixed letters. 1 The five letters ག་ ད་ བ་ མ་ འ་ frequently occur before the real, radical initials of other words, but are seldom pronounced, except in similar cases as § 7. 6. ག་ occurs before ཙ་ ཞ་ ད་ ད་ ན་ ཚ་ ཉ་ ཟ་ ཡ་ ཤ་ ས་ ; ད before the gutturals and labials with exception of the aspiratae; བ་ before ཀ་ ག་, the palatals, dentals and palatal sibilants with the same exception as under ད, then ཉ་ ཟ་ ར་ ཤ་ ས་ ; མ before the gutturals, palatals, dentals and palatal sibilants, excepted the surds; འ before the aspiratae and sonants of the five classes. In C.T., to pronounce them in any case, is considered vulgar. 2. The ambiguity which would arise in case of the prefix standing before one of the 10 final consonants, as single radical, the vowel being the unwritten *a*, — e. g. in the syllable དག་, which, if ད is radical, has to be pronounced *dag*, if prefixed *gā*, — is avoided by adding an འ་ in the latter case: thus, དགའ་. Other examples are: གད་ *gad (gä')* and གདའ་ *dā*; བས་ *bas (bạ, bạ)* and བསའ་ *sā*; མད་ *mad (mä')* and མདའ་ *dā*; འགའ་ *gā*. This འ་ is added, though the radical be not one of the mentioned letters; as, བཀའ་ *kā*. 3. ད as a prefix and བ་ as first radical annul each other, so that only the following sound is heard, as will be seen in the

compound produces in W.T some irregularities, which cannot all be specified here (see the diction . The custom of C.T., according to which the ས་ is entirely neglected is in this instance easier to be followed.

following examples (དབང་ etc.). 4. Another irregularity
is the nasal pronunciation of the prefixed འ in compounds
after a vowel, which is often heard e. g. དགེ་འདུན་ pronounced
gen-dún, *gen-dų́n*, but eleg.: *ge-dún*, ‚clergy‘; བཀའ་འབུམ་
kam-bum, eleg. *ka-búm*, ‚the 100 000 precepts‘ (title of a
book). — *Note*. With regard to the aspiration of the soft
consonants in ET the prefixed letters have the same in-
fluence as the superadded ones § 7. 9.

Examples.

གཡག་ *yag*, bos grunniens.	དཀར་པོ་ *kár-po*, white.
དཔེ་ཆ་ *pé-ča* (Ld: *spe-ča*), book.	དགྲ་བོ་ *ḍá-wo*, enemy.
བཟང་པོ་ *zán-po*, good.	མངར་མོ་ *ṅár-mo*, sweet.
འབབ་པ་ *bab-pa*, to descend.	བཅུ་བཞི་ *čub-ži*, eleg. *ču-ži*, fourteen.
དབང་ *waṅ*, vulg. C: *aṅ*, power.	དབུ་ *u*, resp. head.
དབུས་ *Ú*, name of the Lhasa district.	དབུགས་ *ug(s)*, C: *ug*, *ū*, breath.
དབེན་པ་ *en-pa*, solitude.	དབྱར་ཀ་ *yar-ka*, summer.
དབྱིབས་ *yib(s)*, *ib*, figure.	དབྱེ་བ་ *ye-wa, e-wa*, difference.

9. Word; Accent; Quantity. 1. The peculiarity of the
Tibetan mode of writing in distinctly marking the word-
syllables, but not the words (cf. § 4) composed of two or
more of these, sometimes renders is doubtful what is to be
regarded as one word. 2. There exist a great number of

small monosyllables, which serve for denoting different shades of notions, grammatical relations etc., and are post-poned to the word in question; but never alter its original shape, though their own initials are not seldom influenced by its final consonant (cf. § 15). 3. Such monosyllables may conveniently be regarded as terminations, forming one word together with the preceeding nominal or verbal root. 4. The accent is, in such cases, most naturally given to the root, or, in compounds, generally to the latter part of the composition, as: མིག་ *mig*, ‚eye‘, མིག་གི་ *míg-gi*, ‚of the eye‘; ལག་ *lag*, ‚hand‘, ལག་ཤུབས་ *lag-šub(s)*, ‚hand-covering, glove‘. — 5. Equally natural is, in W.T., the quantity of the vowels: accentuated vowels, when closing the syllable, are comparatively long (though never so long as in the English words *bee*, *stay*, or Hindi لاڑ etc.), otherwise short, as མི་ *mī* ‚man‘, མི་ལ་ *mī-lă* ‚to the man‘, but མར་ *măr*, ‚butter‘. — In CT, however, even accentuated and closing vowels are uttered very shortly: *mĭ*, *mĭ-lă* etc., and long ones occur there only in the case of § 5, 4. 5. and 8, 2., as ལས་ *lạ* ‚work‘; ཆོས་ *čọ* ‚religion‘; མདའ་ *dā* ‚arrow‘; གཟའ་ *zā* ‚planet‘; and in Lhasa especially: ནགས་ *nā* ‚forest‘; ལེགས་པ་ *lē-pa* ‚good‘; རིགས་ *rī* ‚class, sort‘; ཕྱོགས་ *lŏ* ‚side‘; ལུགས་ *lū* ‚manner‘. — In Sanscrit words the long vowels are marked by an འ beneath the conso-nant, as: ནཱམ་ (नाम) ‚called‘, མཱུལ་ (मूल) ‚root‘ (s. § 3).

10. Punctuation. For separating the members of a longer period, a vertical stroke: |, called འཤད་ *šad* (*šă'*), is used, which corresponds at once to our comma, semicolon and colon; after the closing of a sentence the same is doubled; after a longer piece, e g. a chapter, four *šads* are put. No marks of interrogation or exlamation exist in punctuation. — 2. In metrical compositions, the double *šad* is used for separating the single verses; in that case the logical partition of the sentence is not marked (cf. § 4).

A list of a few useful words.

གར་ or ཁར་ *ká-ra, ká-ra,* sugar.

ཁང་པ་ *kaṅ-pa,* house.

གང་ W: *gaṅ,* C: *ǵaṅ,* which?

གུར་ W: *gur,* C: *ǵur,* tent.

ངལ་ *ṅal,* fatigue.

ཅི་ *či,* what?

ཆད་པ་ W: *čad-pa,* C: *čă'-pa,* punishment.

ཆུང་བ་ *čuṅ-wa,* little.

ཇ་ W: *ja,* C: *j'a,* tea.

ཉི་མ་ *ñi-ma,* sun; day.

ཉུང་མ་ *ñuṅ-ma,* turnip.

ཏིབ་རིལ་ *tib-ril,* tea-pot, kettle.

ཀུན་ W: *kun,* C: *kün,* all.

ཁུང་ *kuṅ,* hole.

གརུ་ or གར་ W: *ga-ru, gar,* C: *g°,* where?

ངན་པ་ *ṅan-pa,* C: *ṅam-pa,* bad.

ཆང་ *čaṅ,* beer.

ཆར་པ་ *čár-pa,* rain.

ཆེན་པོ་ *čen-po,* great.

ཉ་ *ña,* fish.

ཉུང་བ་ *ñuṅ-wa,* little, few.

ཉེ་མོ་ *ñe-mo,* near.

དོག་ཙེ་ *tóg-tse* (W), hoe.

ཐག་པ་ *tag-pa*, rope.

སྟོད་པ་ W: *tód-pa*, C: *tö'-pa*, skull.

དང་ *dan, ďan*, and; with.

ནག་པོ་ *nag-po*, black.

ནོར་ *nor*, wealth, property.

ཕན་པ་ *ṕan-pa, ṕäm-pa*, use, benefit.

བ་ *ba, ƀa*, cow.

བུ་ *bu, ƀu*, son.

མེ་ *me*, fire.

མེད་ *med, mě'*, there is not.

ཚང་མ་ *tsan-ma*, whole.

ཞོ་ *žo, šǒ*, curdled milk.

འོད་ *od, wö'*, light, shine.

ཡི་གེ་ *yi-ge*, letter.

ཡོད་ *yod, yö'*, am, is, are.

རི་ *ri*, hill, mountain.

ལ་ *la*, mountain-pass.

ལུག་ *lug*, sheep.

ཐང་ *tán*, the plain.

ད་ W: *da*, C: *ďa*, now.

དུད་པ་ *dud-pa, ďü'-pa*, smoke.

ནད་ *nad, nä'*, disease.

པར་མ་ *ṕár-ma*, a printed book.

ཕུག་རོན་ *ṕug-rón, -rǫn*, dove.

བལ་ *bal, ƀal*, wool.

བུ་མོ་ *bu-mo, ƀ°*, daughter.

མིང་ *min*, name.

ཚམ་ *tsam*, how much?

ཞག་ *žag*, C: *šag*, day.

འོ་མ་ *o-ma, wo-ma*, milk.

ཡང་ *yan*, also.

ཡིན་ *yin*, am, is, are (cf. § 39).

རམ་ *ra-ma*, goat.

རིན་ *rin*, price.

ལམ་ *lam*, road.

ཤ་ *ša*, flesh, meat.

ཤིང་ *šiṅ*, tree, wood.

སུ་ *su*, who?

ཨ་པ་ *a-pa*, (vulg.) father.

རས་ (Ld: *ras*) *rā̤*, cotton cloth.

གོས་ (Ld: *gos*) *gö̤*, *g̈ö̤*, clothing.

སེམས་ *sem*, soul.

ཁྲག་ *ṭag*, blood.

སླེབ་པ་ *leb-pa*, to arrive.

རྩ་ W: *sa*, C: *tsa*, grass.

སྔོན་པོ་ *ñon-po*, *ñom-po*, blue.

གཞུ་ *žu*, bow (for shooting).

དགུན་ཀ་ *gun-ka*, *gun-ka*, winter.

མཚོ་ *tso*, lake.

འདྲི་བ་ *ḍi-wa*, to ask.

ས་ *sa*, earth.

སོ་མ་ *só-ma*, new.

ཨ་མ་ *a-ma* (vulg.) mother.

དུས་ (Ld: *dus*) *dṳ̈*, *d̈ṳ̈*, time.

ཐབས་ *ṭab(s)*, means.

བག་ཕྱེ་ W: *bag-pe*, C: *bag-če*, flour.

གྲོ་ *ḍo*, *d̈ŏ*, wheat.

རྒད་པོ་ *gad-po*, *g̈ä'-po*, old.

སྐྱེ་བ་ *(s)kye-wa*, to be born, grow.

སྙིང་ *ñiṅ*, heart.

གཟིག་ *zig*, leopard.

མགྱོགས་ *gyog(s)-pa* (Ü: *gyō-pa*), fast, quick.

འབྲི་བ་ *ḍi-wa* (*bri-wa*), to write.

Part II.

Etymology.

Chapter I. The Article.

11. Peculiarities of the Tibetan article. 1. What have been called Articles by Csoma and Schmidt, are a number of little affixes: པ་ བ་ མ་ པོ་ བོ་ མོ་, and some similar ones, which might perhaps be more adequately termed denominators, since their principal object is undoubtedly to represent a given root as a noun, substantive or adjective, as is most clearly perceptible in the instance of the roots of verbs, to which པ་ or བ་ impart the notion of the Infinitive and Participle, or the nearest abstract and nearest concrete nouns that can possibly be formed from the idea of a verb. These affixes are not, however, — except in this case — essential to a noun, as many substantives and adjectives and most of the pronouns are never accompanied by them, and even those which usually appear connected with them, will drop them upon the slightest occasion. 2. Almost the only case in which a syntactical use of them, like that of the English definite Article, is perceptible, is that mentioned § 20. 3; a formal one, that of distinguishing the Gender, occurs in a limited number of words, where མོ་ denotes the female, པོ་ the masculine.

Thus: རྒྱལ་པོ་ *gyál-po* ‚king‘, རྒྱལ་མོ་ *gyál-mo* ‚queen‘. Or,

if the word in the masculine (or rather common) gender has
no article, ཨོ is added: སེང་གེ *sén-ge* ‚lion‘, སེང་གེ་མོ
‚lioness‘. 3. In most instances, by far, their only use is
to distinguish different meanings of homonymous roots, e.g.
སྟོན་པ *(s)tón-pa (tón-pa)* ‚teacher‘; སྟོན་མོ *(s)tón-mo (tón-
mo)*, ‚feast‘; སྟོན་ཁ *(s)tón-ka (tón-ka)* ‚autumn‘. Even this
advantage, however, is given up, as soon as a composition
takes place, and then the meaning can only be inferred
from the context, or known from usage: མིང་སྟོན (from
སྟོན་མོ) ‚name feast‘ (given on the occasion of naming or
christening an infant); སྟོན་ཟླ (from སྟོན་ཁ) ‚autumnal
month‘. In some instances the putting or omitting of these
articles is optional; more frequently the usage varies in
different provinces. 4. The peculiar nature of these affixes
is most clearly shown by the manner in which they are
connected with the indefinite article § 13.

Note. The affixes བ་ བོ are after vowels and after
the consonants ང་ ར་ ལ always pronounced *wa* and *wo*,
instead of *ba* and *bo*; thus, དཀའ་བ *ka-wa* ‚difficult‘; རེ་བ
re-wa ‚hope‘; གང་བ *gaṅ-wa (gh°)* ‚full‘; ཟེར་བ *zer-wa
(ser-wa)* ‚to say‘; དམྱལ་བ *nyal-wa* ‚hell‘; ཇོ་བོ *jo-wo (jho-
wo)* ‚lord, master‘.

12. Difference of the Articles among each other. 1. The
usage of པ་ བ་ མ is the most general and widest of all,

as they occur with all sorts of substantives and other nouns. པ་ is particularly used for denoting a man who is in a certain way connected with a certain thing (something like یٖ, and جا in Hindustāni and Persian: གྲྭ་ *ḍa* ‚school‘, གྲྭ་པ་ (literally: scholar) ‚disciple, novice‘; ཆུ་ *ču*, ‚water‘, ཆུ་པ་ ‚water-carrier‘ (یٖ, اب); རྟ་ ‚horse‘, རྟ་པ་ ‚horseman‘; དབུས་ ‚the province of Ū‘, དབུས་པ་ ‚a man from Ū‘, ཁྱེའུ་ *kyëu* ‚boy‘, ལོ་ *lo* ‚year‘, གཉིས་ *ñi(s)* ‚two‘, hence: ཁྱེའུ་ལོ་གཉིས་པ་ ‚a two years’ boy‘. If the feminine is required མ་ is either added to, or — more commonly — used instead of, the former: དབུས་མ་ ‚a woman from Ū‘; བུ་མོ་ལོ་གཉིས་མ་ ‚a two years’ girl‘. The performer of an action is more frequently denoted by པོ་ (or, in more solemn language, པ་པོ་), though, in conversation at least, མཁན་ *k̲an* (*k̲en*), is preferred; བྱེད་པ་ *jed-pa* ‚to do, make; doing, making‘: བྱེད་པོ་, བྱེད་པ་པོ་, བྱེད་མཁན་ ‚the doer, maker‘. 2. The appendices ཀ་ ཁ་ ག་ occur with a limited number of nouns only, especially the names of the seasons, with numerals, and some pronouns. (གོ་ seems to be a vulgar form of pronunciation for ཀ་).

13. The indefinite Article. This is the numeral one (§ 13), only deprived of its prefix, viz: ཅིག་, which form it retains, if the preceding word ends with ག་ ད་ བ་, as: ཁབ་ཅིག་

k̃ab-čig, a needle; it is changed to ཞིག་ after ས་, རས་ཞིག་ *ras-šig*, *rä-šig*, a cloth; to ཞིག་ *žig (šig)* in all other cases. Some authors use ཅིག་ after any termination indisriminately. It is, of course, always without accent. The articles པ་ བ་ etc. are not thrown out by the indefinite article e.g. སྟོན་པ་ ,teacher, the teacher', སྟོན་པ་ཞིག་ ,a teacher'. It is used even after a plurality: thus, ཆུ་མིག་བཞི་ཞིག་རེ་ཙུ་ཡོད་ ,there were some four wells', and even: མང་ཞིག་གདའ་སྟེ་ ,there being a multitude of them' (from Mil). Very often it is placed after the interrogative pronouns (v. 27), and sometimes its original meaning is obscured so much that it occurs even after known and definite subjects, where one would expect the demonstrative (see f. i. Dzl. 25, 1. 28, 6. 128, 14).

Chapter II. The Substantive.

14. The Number. The Plural is denoted by adding the word རྣམས་ *nam,* or, more rarely, དག་ *dag (d'ag)*, ཚོ་, or a few other words, which originally were nouns with the common notion of plurality. But this mark of the Plural is usually omitted, when the plurality of the thing in question may be known from other circumstances, e. g. when a numeral is added: thus, མི་ ,man', མི་རྣམས་ ,men', མི་གསུམ་ ,three men'. When a substantive is connected with an adjective, the plural sign is added only once, viz. after the last of the connected words: མི་བཟང་པོ་རྣམས་ ‚the good men‘.

Note. The conversational language uses the words རྣམས་ etc. seldom, in WT scarcely ever (an exception s. 24. Remarks), but add, when necessary, such words as: all, many, some; two, three, seven, eight, or other suitable numerals (cf. § 20, 5.).

15. Declension. The regular addition of the different particles or single sounds by which the cases are formed is the same for all nouns, whether substantives or adjectives, pronouns or participles. Only in some cases, in the Dative and Instrumental, the noun itself is changed, when, ending in an vowel, it admits of a closer connection with the corrupted case-sign. We may reckon in Tibetan seven cases, expressive of all the relations, for which cases are used in other languages, viz nominative and accusative, genitive, instrumental, dative, locative, ablative, terminative and vocative. 1. The unaltered form of the noun has some of the functions of our Nominative and those of the Accusative and Vocative. 2. The sign of the Genitive is ཀྱི་ after words with the finals ད་ བ་ ས་ ; གྱི་ after ན་ མ་ ར་ ལ་, གི་ after ག་ and ང་; after vowels *i* is simply added by means of an འ་ thus: འི་, which then will form a diphthong with the vowel of the noun (cf. § 6), or if, in versification, two syllables are required, *i* appears supported by an ཡ་ forming a distinct word. 3. The Instrumental or Agent is expressed by the particles ཀྱིས་ གྱིས་ or གིས་ after the respective consonants as specified above; after vowels simply ས་ is added, or, in verse, sometimes ཡིས་

Note. The instrumental is, in modern pronunciation, except in Northern Ladak, scarcely discernible from the genitive, and there are but few if any, even among lamas, who are not liable to confound both cases in writing.

In the language of common life, in WT, the different forms of the particle of the genitive and instrumental, after consonants, གྱི་ གྱི་ etc. are never heard, but everywhere the final consonant is doubled and the vowel *i* added to it, thus: ལུས་, G. *lus-si* (Ld.), *lū-i*; ལམ་ G. *lam-mi*; གསེར་ (gold), G. *ser-ri* etc.; or, in other words, all nouns ending in consonants are formed like those ending with ག་ (see the example ཤིག་). In those ending with a vowel no irregularity takes place.

4. The Dative adds indiscriminately the postposition ལ་ *la*, denoting the relation of space in the widest sense, expressed by the English prepositions *in, into, at, on, to.*
5. The Locative is formed by the postposition ན་ *na* ,in‘.

6. The Ablative by ནས་ *na̧* or ལས་ *la̧* ,from‘ (the latter especially with the meaning: *from among*), all three likewise without any discriminating regard to the ending of the noun. 7. The Terminative is expressed by the postpositions རུ་ or ར་ after vowels; ཏུ་ after final ག་ and བ་ and, in certain words, ད་ ར་ ལ་ ; སུ་ after ས་ ; དུ་ generally after ན་ ར་ ལ་ and the other final consonants. All these

postpositions denote the movement *to* or *into*. 8. The Vocative is not different from the Nominative (as stated above), if not distinguished by the interjection ཀྱེ *oh!*, and can only be known from the context.

Examples of declension. As example of the declension of consonontal nouns we may take 1. for those in *s* (respectively *d*, *b*), ལུས་ *lus, lū*, ‚body‘; 2. for those in *m* (*n*, *r*, *l*), ལམ་ *lam* ‚way‘; 3. for those in *g* (*ṅ*), མིག་ *mig* ‚eye‘, — of that of vocalic nouns: 4. ཁ་ *ka* or *ka-wa* ‚snow‘.

S i n g u l a r.

	1.		2.
N. Acc.	ལུས་ *lus, lū*		ལམ་ *lam*
Gen.	ལུས་ཀྱི་ *lus-kyi, lū-kyi;* *lus-si, lūi*		ལམ་གྱི་ *lam-gyi; lam-mi*
Inst.	ལུས་ཀྱིས་ *lus-kyis, lū-kyī;* *lus-sī, lūī*		ལམ་གྱིས་ *lam-gyis, -gyī;* *lam-mī*
Dat.	ལུས་ལ་ *lus-la, lū-la*		ལམ་ལ་ *lam-la*
Loc.	ལུས་ན་ *lus-na*		ལམ་ན་ *lam-na*
Abl.	ལུས་ནས་ *lus-nā*		ལམ་ནས་ *lam-nā*
Term.	ལུས་སུ་ *lus-su*		ལམ་དུ་ *lam-du*

	3.		4.
N. Acc.	མིག་ *mig*		ཁ་ *ka;* ཁ་བ་ *ka-wa*
Gen.	མིག་གི་ *mig-gi*		ཁའི་ *kai;* ཁ་བའི་ *ka-wai*

Inst.	མིག་གིས་ *mig-gis, -gī*	ཁས་ *k͟ā*;	ཁ་བས་ *k͟a-wā*
Dat.	མིག་ལ་ *mig-la*	ཁ་ལ་ *k͟a-la*;	ཁ་བ་ལ་ *k͟a-wa-la*
Loc.	མིག་ན་ *mig-na*	ཁ་ན་ *k͟a-na*;	ཁ་བ་ན་ *k͟a-wa-na*
Abl.	མིག་ནས་ *mig-nā*	ཁ་ནས་ *k͟a-nā̤*;	ཁ་བ་ནས་ *k͟a-wa-nā̤*
Term.	མིག་ཏུ་ *mig-tu*	ཁ་རུ་, ཁར་ *k͟a-ru, k͟ar*;	
		ཁ་བ་རུ་, ཁ་བར་	
		k͟a-wa-ru,	*k͟a-war.*

Plural.

As the plural signs are simply added to the nouns, without affecting their form, we here only give examples of declension with the two most frequent plural particles. As example for དག་ the plural of the pron. དེ་ ‚that‘ has been chosen.

N. Acc.	ལུས་རྣམས་ *lus(lü̈-)-nam(s)*	དེ་དག་ *de-dag*	
Gen.	ལུས་རྣམས་ཀྱི་ *lus-nam(s)-kyi*	དེ་དག་གི་ *de-dag-gi*	
Inst.	ལུས་རྣམས་ཀྱིས་ *lus-nam(s)-kyis*	དེ་དག་གིས་ *de-dag-gis*	
Dat.	ལུས་རྣམས་ལ་ *lus-nam(s)-la*	དེ་དག་ལ་ *de-dag-la*	
Loc.	ལུས་རྣམས་ན་ *lus-nam(s)-na*	དེ་དག་ན་ *de-dag-na*	
Abl.	ལུལ་རྣམས་ནས་ *lus-nam(s)-nā̤*	དེ་དག་ནས་ *de-dag-nā̤*	
Term.	ལུས་རྣམས་སུ་ *lus-nam(s)-su*	དེ་དག་ཏུ་ *de-dag-tu*	

Chapter III.
The Adjective.

16. In the Tibetan language the Adjective is not form-
ally distinguished from the Substantive, so that many nouns
may be used one or the other way just as circumstances
require.*) The declension, likewise, follows the same rules
as that of substantives   Only two remarks may be added
here. 1. The particles པ་ མ་ པོ་ མོ་ are not very strictly
used for distinguishing the gender, since even in the case
of human beings པ་ and པོ་ are not seldom found connected
with feminines, e. g.: བུ་མོ་མཛེས་པ་ just as well as བུ་མོ་
མཛེས་མ་ „a fine girl‘. 2. The Adjective stands after the
Substantive to which it belongs: thus, རི་མཐོན་པོ་ *ri-tón-
po*, C: *ri-ṭon-po*, „the high hill‘, when, of course, the case-

---

*) But the vulgar language has a predilection for certain forms
of Adjectives 1. those with the gerundial particle དེ་, as: ཚན་དེ་
for the more classical ཚན་ ‘„warm‘; these seem to be particularly
in use in Tsan: མཛེན་སྟེ་ „friendly‘, less so in Ü. 2. compound adjectives either by simple reiteration of the root: རིལ་རིལ་ for
རིལ་པོ་ „round‘, or changing the vowel at the same time: ཁྲག་ཁྲུག་
„complicate‘, གཙང་གཙོང་ awry etc Often they are quadrisyllables
after this form: སླལ་ལ་སྐྱུལ་ལེ་ „lukewarm‘, ཚག་ག་ཚོག་གི་ „medley‘.

signs are joined to the Adjective: རི་མཐོན་པོ་དེ་ ,of the high hill', རི་མཐོན་པོ་རྣམས་ ,the high hills' etc.

Or the Adjective may be put in the Gen. before the Substantive: མཐོན་པོ་དེ་རི་ , and then the latter only is declined: མཐོན་པོ་དེ་རིའི་ , མཐོན་པོ་དེ་རི་རྣམས་ . In the vulgar speech both of C and WT the adjective sometimes preserves, even in this position, its simple form (Nominative). A third way of expression, when both are joined together, without any article, as སྐམ་ས་ instead of ས་སྐམ་པོ་ the dry land, is rather a compound substantive, with the same difference of meaning as ,highland' and ,a high land' in English.

17. Comparison. 1. Special endings, expressive of the different degrees of comparison, as in the Aryan languages, do not exist in Tibetan. There are two particles, however, corresponding to the English *than*: བས་ , after the final consonants ང་ ར་ ལ་ and after vowels (པས་ , after ག་ ད་ ན་ བ་ མ་ ས་ *)), and ལས་ ; these particles follow the word with which another is compared (like the Hind. سے) and this then preceeds the compared one, finally follows the adjective in the positive: རྟ་བས་ (or ལས་) ཁྱི་ཆུང་བ་ཡིན་ ,horse — than dog small is', just as in Hindūstāni: گھوڑی سی کتّا چھوٹا ہی . But also the position usual in

---

*) Some Mscr. and wood-prints, however, prefer, even after these consonants, the form བས་ .

our European languages occurs, thus: རབ་ཏུ་འབྱུང་བའི་ བསོད་ནམས་རི་རབ་ལྷུན་པོ་བས་འཕངས་མཐོ་ཉོ་ ‚the merit of becoming a priest is relatively higher that mount Meru‘; བོད་ཀྱི་རྒྱལ་པོ་གཞན་ལས་ཆེ་བ་ཡིན་ནོ་ ‚the king of Tibet is greater than the other ones‘. The particle བས་ (པས་) may be put, in the same manner, after adverbs. Thus, སྔར་ བས་གསལ་བར་མཐོང་བར་གྱུར་ཏོ་ ‚(their eyes) became more keen-sighted than before‘. Or, after infinitives, གཞན་སོང་ བ་བས་ནུ་བོས་སོང་ན་ཐན་ ‚it is better (for him) that his younger brother should go (with him) than another‘. ལས་ for it-self has the meaning of ‚more than‘, with the negative: ‚not more than‘, ‚only‘; thus: ང་ལ་སྲང་གཉིས་ལས་ནི་མི་དགོས་ ‚more than two ounces I do not want‘ (cf. vulg. WT: གསུམ་ མན་ན་མེད་ ‚there are not more than (only) three‘); or ‚noth-ing but‘, ‚only‘, རི་དྭགས་ཉོར་བ་ལས་དགའ་བ་མེད་ ‚there is no pleasure (for us) but hunting, h. is our only pl‘.

   2. An Adverb which augments the notion of the ad-jective itself, is ལྷག་པར་ ‚more‘; this can be added ad li-bitum: ད་བས་ཀྱི་ལྷག་པར་ཆུང་བ་ཡིན་.

   3. Another adverb, ཇེ་ means: ‚more and more‘, ‚gra-dually more‘, e. g. ཇེ་ཉེ་ཇེ་ཉེ་སོང་སྟེ་ ‚going nearer and nearer‘.
   4. ‚The elder — the younger‘ e. g. of two brothers, is

simply expressed by: ,the great — the little'. 5. The
Superlative is paraphrased by the same means: གུན་ལས་
ཆེན་པོ་ or ཐམས་ཅད་པས་ཆེན་པོ་ ,greater than all'. Or it is
expressed in the following manner: ཡུལ་གྱི་རྒྱལ་པོ་འི་ནང་ན་
རྒྱལ་པོ་གང་ཆེ་ ,of (among) the kings of the country which
one is the greatest (prop. great)?'. Adverbs for expressing
high degrees are: ཤིན་ཏུ་ or རབ་ཏུ་ ,very', གུན་ཏུ་ ,all',
ཨོངས་སུ་ ,quite', མཆོག་ཏུ་ ,exceedingly' etc.

Note. The colloquial language of WT uses སང་ instead of བས་ or ལས་, and མ་ (*mā*, always with a strong
emphasis, perhaps a mutilated form of མང་ས་ ,much') or
མང་པོ་ instead of ཤིན་ཏུ་, whereas that of CT employs ལས་
in the former case, but repeats the adjective in the latter,
so that ,very large' is expressed in books by ཤིན་ཏུ་ཆེན་པོ་,
in speaking, in WT by *má čén-po*, in CT by *čem-po čem-po*.

Chapter IV.
The Numerals.

18. Cardinals:

1   *੨*   གཅིག་ *čig*

2   *੩*   གཉིས་ *ñi(s)*

3   *੩*   གསུམ་ *sum*

4   ༔   བཞི་ *ži*

5   ༥   ལྔ་ *ṅa*

6   ༦   དྲུག་ W: *ḍug*, C: *ḍhug*

7   ༧   བདུན་ W: *dun*, C: *dhụn*

8   ༨   བརྒྱད་ W: *gyad*, C: *gyä'*

9   ༩   དགུ་ *gu*

10   ༡༠   བཅུ་ *ču*, or བཅུ་ཐམ་པ་ *ču-ťam-pa*

11   ༡༡   བཅུ་གཅིག་ *ču-čig*

12   ༡༢   བཅུ་གཉིས་ *ču-ñi*, vulg: * čug-ñi(s)*

13   ༡༣   བཅུ་གསུམ་ *ču-súm*, vulg: *čug-súm*

14   ༡༔   བཅུ་བཞི་ *ču-ži*, vulg: *čub-ži*

15   ༡༥   བཅོལྔ་ *čo-ṅá*

16   ༡༦   བཅུ་དྲུག་ *ču-ḍúg*, C: *-ḍhúg*

17   ༡༧   བཅུ་བདུན་ *ču-dún*, C: *-dụ́n*, vulg: *čub-dˢ*

18   ༡༨   བཅོབརྒྱད་ *čo-gyád*, C: *-gyä'*, vulg: *čob-gˢ*

19   ༡༩   བཅུ་དགུ་ *ču-gú*

20   ༢༠   ཉི་ཤུ་ *ñi-śu*

21   ༢༡   ཉི་ཤུ་རྩ་གཅིག་ *ñi-śu-sa-čig*, or ཉེར་གཅིག་ *ñer-čig*

30 ༣༠ སུམ་ཅུ་ *súm-ču*

31 ༣༡ སུམ་ཅུ་རྩ་གཅིག་ *sum-ču-sa-čig*, སོ་གཅིག་ *so-čig*

40 ༤༠ བཞི་བཅུ་ *ži-ču*, vulg: *žib-ču*

41 ༤༡ བཞི་བཅུ་རྩ་གཅིག་ *ži-ču-sa-čig*, ཞེ་གཅིག་ *že-čig*

50 ༥༠ ལྔ་བཅུ་ *ṅa-ču*, vulg: *ṅab-ču*

51 ༥༡ ལྔ་བཅུ་རྩ་གཅིག་ *ṅa-ču-sa-čig*, ང་གཅིག་ *ṅa-čig*

60 ༦༠ དྲུག་ཅུ་ *ḍug-ču*, C: *ḍhug-ču*

61 ༦༡ དྲུག་ཅུ་རྩ་གཅིག་ *ḍug-ču-sa-čig*, རེ་གཅིག་ *re-čig*

70 ༧༠ བདུན་ཅུ་ *dun-ču*, C: *dṵn-ču*

71 ༧༡ བདུན་ཅུ་རྩ་གཅིག་ *dun-ču-sa-čig*, དོན་གཅིག་ *don-čig*

80 ༨༠ བརྒྱད་ཅུ་ *gyád-ču*, C: *gyä̀-ču*

81 ༨༡ བརྒྱད་ཅུ་རྩ་གཅིག་ *gyad-ču-sa-čig*, གྱ་གཅིག་ *gya-čig*

90 ༩༠ དགུ་བཅུ་ *gú-ču*, vulg: *gúb-ču*

91 ༩༡ དགུ་བཅུ་རྩ་གཅིག་ *gu-ču-sa-čig*, གོ་གཅིག་ *go číg* (C: *ǵo-čig*)

100 ༡༠༠ བརྒྱ་(ཐམ་པ་) *gya* (*tám-pa*)

101 ༡༠༡ བརྒྱ་དང་གཅིག་ or བརྒྱ་རྩ་གཅིག་ *gya daṅ* (or *sa*) *čig*

200 ༢༠༠ ཉི་བརྒྱ་ *ñi-gya*, vulg: *ñib-gya*

300 ༣༠༠ སུམ་བརྒྱ་ *sum-gya*

400	⅄∞	བཞི་བརྒྱ་	*ži-gya*, vulg: *žib-gya* etc.
1000	⁍∞∞	སྟོང་	(s)*toń*
10 000	⁍∞ ∞∞	ཁྲི་	*ṭi*
100 000	⁍∞∞ ∞∞∞	འབུམ་	*bum*
1 000 000	⁍ ∞∞∞ ∞∞∞	ས་ཡ་	*sa-ya*
10 000 000	⁍∞ ∞∞∞ ∞∞∞	བྱེ་བ་	*je-wa*

There are, as in Sanscrit, names for many more powers of 10, but they are seldom used.

19. Ordinals. དང་པོ་ W: *dań-po*, C: *d°* ‚the first‘, the rest are simply formed by adding པ་ to the cardinals, as: གཉིས་པ་, the second etc.; the 21. is ཉི་ཤུ་རྩ་གཅིག་པ་ ‚the twenty-oneth‘, not, as in English, ‚the twenty first‘.

20. Remarks. 1. The smaller number postponed indicates, as is seen in § 18, addition, the reverse — multiplication: བཅུ་གསུམ་ 13, གསུམ་ཅུ་ 30; but in the latter case the three first numerals are changed to ཆིག་, ཉི་, གསུམ་; and བཅུ་, as the second part of a compound after consonants, is spelled ཅུ་. 2. The words ཐམ་པ་ (after full tens up to one hundred), སྒ་ (after hundreds and thousands*)),

----

*) སྒ་ is used especially if the number counting the hundreds,

ཚོ་ (with still greater numbers), are optional but frequent additions. རྩ་ is common instead of དང་ ‚and', to connect units with tens (s. § 18), but it occurs also with hundreds and thousands, and not seldom together with དང་, e.g. སྟོང་ དང་རྩ་གཉིས་, 1002. It is used also instead of ཐམ་པ་, as: བཅུ་ རྩ་ ten, ཉི་ཤུ་རྩ་ twenty; often it is standing alone for ཉི་ཤུ་རྩ་, as: རྩ་གཉིས་, twenty two. This latter custom may have caused the belief, common even among educated readers in C and WT, that རྩ་ must mean twenty, even when connecting a hundred or thousand to a unit, as they will usually understand the above mentioned number in the sense of 1022 instead of 1002; but the authority of printed books, wherever the exact number can be verified from other circumstances, does not confirm this, which would indeed be a sadly ambiguous phraseology. 3. ཀ་ added to a cardinal number means conjunction: གཉིས་ཀ་, the two together, both; གསུམ་ཀ་, the three together, all three etc. པོ་ means either the same, or represents the definite article, indicating that the number has been already mentioned, e.g. མི་ལྔ་ ··· བཏང་ངོ་། །མི་ལྔ་པོ་བསླེབ་སྟེ་ ···, five men were sent ... The five men arriving etc. 4. བ་ is used, besides

_____

thousands etc. follows: thus, སྟོང་ཕྲག་ཉི་ཤུ ‚of thousands: twenty, 20 000'; ཁྲི་ཕྲག་དུ་མ་ ‚many ten-thousands'.

forming Ordinals, to express the notion of ‚containing‘, e. g.
ཨེ་གོ་དྲུག་པ་ ‚that containing six letters‘, viz. the famous
formula: ཨོཾ་མ་ཎི་པ་དྨེ་ཧཱུྃ om maṇi padme hum; སུམ་ཅུ་པ་,
‚that containing thirty (letters)‘, the Tibetan alphabet.
5. Such combinations as གཉིས་གསུམ་ etc. are frequently
used in common life, so denote a number approximately,
‚two or three or so‘ (cf. § 14 Note).

21. Distributive numerals. They are expressed by repe-
tition as in Hind: དྲུག་དྲུག་ each time six, six for each etc.
In composed numerals only the last member is repeated,
thus སུམ་ཅུ་ར་གཉིས་གཉིས་ each time thirty two.

22. Adverbial numerals. 1. Firstly, secondly etc. are
formed from the ordinals as every Adverb is from an Adjective, viz. by adding the letter ར་, དང་པོར་, གཉིས་པར་
etc. (s. § 41). 2. Multiplicative adverbs, ‚once‘, ‚twice‘ etc.,
are expressed by putting ལན་ ‚times‘ before the cardinal:
ལན་གཅིག་, ལན་གཉིས་, W: *lan-čig, lan-ñi(s)*, C: *län-čig,
län-ñī* ‚once, twice‘ etc.; seldom ཆོར་, ཚར་, ཐེངས་ with the
same meaning as ལན་.

23. Fractional numerals are formed by adding ཆ་ ‚part‘:
thus, བརྒྱའི་ཆ་ ‚a hundredth part‘ etc., but also: བང་མཛོད་
གསུམ་ཆ་ཞིག་ ‚one third of the treasury‘.

Chapter V.

Pronouns.

24. Personal Pronouns. First person: ང་ *ṅa*; ངེད་ *ṅed, ṅĕ'*; ངོས་ *ṅos* (Ld); ཁོ་བོ་ *ḱo-wo*, masc., and ཁོ་མོ་ *ḱo-mo*, fem.; བདག་ *dag* ,self' — ,I'; Second person: ཁྱོད་ *ḱyod* (*ḱyö'*), ཁྱེད་ *ḱyed* (*ḱyĕ'*) ,thou, you'; Third person: ཁོ་ *ḱo*, ཁོང་ *ḱoṅ* — ,he, she, it'.

The plural is formed by adding ཅག་, རྣམས་, ཅག་རྣམས་ or ཚོ་, but very often, if circumstances show the meaning with sufficient certainty, the sign of the plural is altogether omitted. The declension is the same as that of the substantives.

Remarks: ང་ is the most common and can be used by every body; ངེད་ seems to be preferred in elegant speech (s. Note); ངོས་ is very common in modern letter writing, at least in WT; བདག་ ,self', when speaking to superior persons occurs very often in books, but has disappeared from common speech, except in the province of Tsaṅ (*Taśi-lhunpo*) as also the following; ཁོ་བོ་, ཁོ་མོ་ in easy conversation with persons of equal rank, or to inferiors.

2. person. ཁྱོད་ is used in books in addressing even the highest persons, but in modern conversation only among equals or to inferiors; ཁྱེད་ is elegant and respectful, especially in books. —

3. person. ཁོ་ seldom occurs in books, where the demonstr. pron. དེ་ (§ 26) is generally used instead; ཁོང་ is common to both the written and the spoken language, and used, at least in the latter, as respectful. But it must be remarked that the pronoun of the third person is in most cases entirely omitted, even when there is a change of subject. — Instead of ང་ཅག་ and ཁྱེད་ཅག་ the people of WT use ང་ཉ་ and ཁྱོ་ཉ་; the vulgar plural of ཁོ་ is ཁོ་པ་. —

To each of these pronouns may be added: རང་ *rañ* or ཉིད་ *ñid, ñi'* ‚self‘, and in conversational language ང་རང་, ཁྱེད་རང་, ཁོ་རང་ are, perhaps, even more frequently used than the simple forms, without any difference in the meaning. ཉིད་ is more prevalent in books, except the compound ཉིད་རང་ *ñi-rañ*, which is in modern speech the usual respectful pronoun of address, like ‚Sie‘ in German.

Note. The predilection of Eastern Asiatics for a system of ceremonials in the language is met with also in Tibetan. There is one separate class of words, which must be used in reference to the honoured person, when spoken to as well as when spoken of. To this class belong, besides the pronouns ཉིད་རང་, ཁྱེད་, ཁོང་, all the respectful terms by which the body or soul, or parts of the same, and all things or persons pertaining to such a person, and

even his actions, must be called. The notions, most frequently occurring, have special expressions, as སྐུ་ *(s)ku*, instead of ལུས་ *lus, lü̠*, ‚body‘; དབུ་ *u*, i. o. མགོ་ *go* ‚head‘;
ཐུགས་ *tug(s)* (Ü: *tū*), i. o. སེམས་ *sem(s)* ‚soul‘, or ཡིད་
yid, yi̠, ‚mind‘; ཡབ་ *yab*, i. o. པ་ (vulg: ཨ་པ་), ‚father‘;
ན་བཟའ་ *na-za*, i. o. གོས་ *gos, gö̠*, ‚coat‘, ‚dress‘; ཆིབས་
čib(s), i. o. རྟ་ *(r)ta, sta* ‚horse‘; བཞུགས་པ་ *žug(s)-pa* (Ü:
žū-pa), i. o. སྡོད་པ་ *dod-pa, dö̠-pa* ‚to sit‘; མཛད་པ་ *dzad-pa,*
dzä̠-pa i. o. བྱེད་པ་ *jed-pa, jhe̠-pa* ‚to make‘ and many
others. If there is no such special word, any substantive
may be rendered respectful by adding སྐུ་ or ཐུགས་ respectively (so, སྐུ་ཚེ་ i. o. ཚེ་ ‚lifetime‘; ཐུགས་ཁྲོ་བ་ i. o. ཁྲོ་བ་
‚anger‘) any verb by adding མཛད་པ་, according to 39, 1.
Another class of what might be called e l e g a n t terms are
to be used when conversing with an honoured person (or
also by a high person himself in his own speech), such as
བགྱིད་པ་ *gyid-pa, gyi̠-pa* ‚to do‘; མཆིས་པ་ *či-pa*, ‚to be‘;
སླད་དུ་ *lad-du, lä̠-du* i. o. ཕྱིར་དུ་ ‚for the sake of‘, with-
o u t reference to the said person himself. Even uneducated
people know, and make use of, most of the ‚respectful‘
terms, but the merely ‚elegant‘ ones are, at least in WT,
seldom or never heard in conversation.

25. Possessive pronouns. The Possessive is simply

expressed by the Genitive of the Personal, ང་འི་, ཁྱོད་ཀྱི་ etc. ,His‘, ,her‘, ,its‘, when referring to the acting subject˙ (suus), must be expressed by རང་གི་ or ཉིད་ཀྱི་ ,his own‘; otherwise (ejus) by ཁོ་འི་, ཁོང་གི་, དེ་འི་. In C, in the latter case, ང་ཅན་, ཁྱོད་ཅན་, ཁོ་ཅན་ are used.

26. Reflective and Reciprocal pronouns. 1. The Reflective pronoun, ,myself‘, ,yourself˙ etc. is expressed by རང་, ཉིད་, also བདག་. But in the case of the same person being the subject and object of an action, it must be paraphrased, so for ,he precipitated himself from the rock‘ must be said ,he precipitated his own body etc.‘ རང་གི་ལུས་; for ,he rebuked himself‘ — ,he rebuked his own soul‘ རང་གི་སེམས་ — 2. The reciprocal pronoun ,each other‘ or ,one another‘ is rendered by ,one — one‘, as གཅིག་གིས་གཅིག་བསད་ ,by one one was killed‘, ,they killed one another‘; གཅིག་ལ་ གཅིག་ན་རེ་ ,to one one said‘, ,they said to each other‘.

27. Demonstrative pronouns. 1. འདི་ *di*, ,this‘; དེ་ *de*, *dhe* ,that‘ are those most frequently used, both in books and speaking. The Plural is generally formed by དག་, but also by རྣམས་ and ཚོ་. More emphatical are འདི་ཀ་, འདི་ག་, འདི་ཀོ་, འདི་གོ་, ,just this‘, ,this same‘; དེ་ཀ་ etc. ,that same‘. — The vulgar dialect also uses ད་གྱི་ *hǎ-gyi*

and པ་གྱི་ *pǎ-gyi* for ‚that‘, ‚yonder‘, and, in WT, འི་,
འི་རོ་ for ‚this‘ and ཨ་ for ‚that‘; པ་གྱི་ occurs even in
books. — 2. It is worth remarking that the distinction of
the nearer and remoter relation is, even in common language, scrupulously observed. If reference is made to an
object already mentioned, དེ་ is used; if to something following, འདི་; e.g. དེ་སྐད་ཅེས་སྨྲས་སོ་ ‚that speech he said‘,
‚thus he said‘; འདི་སྐད་ཅེས་སྨྲས་པ་ ‚this speech he said‘,
‚he said thus, spoke the following words‘.

28. Interrogative pronouns. They are སུ་ *su* ‚who?‘;
གང་ *gan*, gh. ‚which?‘; ཅི་ *ci* ‚what?‘; to these the indefinite article ཞིག་ is often added, སུ་ཞིག་ etc. The two former
can also assume the plural termination དག་, སུ་དག་, གང་
དག་. — In CT གང་ is frequently used instead of ཅི་

29. Relative pronouns. These are almost entirely want-
ing in the Tibetan language, and our subordinate relative
clauses must be expressed by Participles und Gerunds, or
a new independent sentence must be begun. The participle, in such a case, is treated quite as an adjective, being
put either in the Genitive before the substantive, or, in
the Nominative, after: འགྲོ་བའི་ཚོང་པ་རྣམས་ ‚the merchants
who would go (with him)‘; བྱག་ཐག་གཡུ་བརྒྱུས་པ་ ‚the cord
on which turquoises are strung‘; འཁྲིས་མ་མོང་པོ་ཡོང་བ་ཞིག

‚one who gets (unto whom come) many presents‘. Cf. also
33. Only those indefinite sentences which in English are
introduced by ‚he who‘, ‚who ever‘, ‚that which‘, ‚what‘ etc.
can be adequately expressed in Tibetan, by using the interrogative pronouns with the participle (seldom the naked
root) of the verb, or adding ན་ (‚if —‘ v. 41, A. 4.) to the
latter. Instead of ཅེ་ in this case ཇེ་ is written more cor-
rectly. Thus: སུ་ལ་དམ་པའི་ཆོས་མཆིས་པ་བདག་ལ་སྟོན་པར་
གྱུར་ན་ ‚if anybody who possesses the good faith teach it
me‘; ཁྱོད་སུ་འགྲོ་བ་དག་ཀུང་འགྲོགས་ཏེ་ ‚when those of you
who wish to go are assembled‘; ནོར་བུ་རིན་པོ་ཆེ་འདི་ཇེ་འདོད་
པ་ཐམས་ཅད་ཆར་བཞིན་དུ་འབེབས་སོ་ ‚this jewel (cintāmani)
will make come down like rain whatever is wished for‘;
ཁྱོད་ཅི་ཟེར་ཁྱོད་ཇེ་སྨྲས་པ་བཞིན་དུ་བྱའོ་ ‚whatever you way say
and ask of me according to that I will act, or I will grant
you whatever you ask‘. བདག་གིས་མཐུ་ཇི་ཡོད་པས་རྒྱ་
མཚོའི་ཆུ་བཅུས་ཏེ་ ‚having scooped the water of the sea with
what force I have‘; རིན་པོ་ཆེ་ཇི་ལྟ་བུ་ཞིག་རྙེད་པ་བདག་ལ་
བསྟན་དུ་གསོལ་ ‚I beg you to show me what sort of jewel
you have found (got)‘; རྐང་གྱི་རྗེས་གང་རིགས་པར་གསེར་གྱི་
བྱེ་མར་གྱུར་ཏོ་ ‚his footprints, in what place soever they fell
(v. lex. s. v. རིགས་), became gold-sand‘.

But the participle is treated as if no relative was preceding, thus སྔར་རྗེ་སྐད་སྨྲས་པ་ལས་མ་ལྡོགས་སོ་ ,he did not
recede from (recall) the word he had spoken before'; vulg.,
WT, ང་གང་བསྡད་པའི་ཁང་མིག ,the room where I sat'.

Chapter VI.

The Verb.

30. Introductory remarks. The Tibetan verb must be
regarded as denoting, not an action, or suffering, or condition of any subject, but merely a coming to pass, or,
in other words, they are all impersonal verbs, like *taedet*,
miseret etc. in Latin, or *it suits* etc. in English. Therefore
they are destitute of what is called in our own languages
the active and passive voice, as well as of the discrimi-
nation of persons, and show nothing beyond a rather poor
capability of expressing the most indispensable distinctions
of tense and mood. From the same reason the acting
subject of a transitive verb must regularly appear in the
Instrumental case, as the case of the subject of a neutral
verb,— which, in European languages, is the Nominative —,
ought to be regarded, from a Tibetan point of view, as
Accusative expressing the object of an impersonal verb,
just as ,poenitet me' is translated by ,I repent'. But it
will perhaps be easier to say: The subject of a transitive
verb, in Tibetan, assumes regularly the form of the instrumental, of a neutral verb that of the nominative which
is the same as the accusative. Thus, ངས་ཁོང་རྡུང་ is pro-

perly: རྡུང་ a beating happens, ཁྱོད་ regarding you, ངས་ by me = I beat you. In common life the object has often the form of the dative, ཁྱོད་ལ་, to facilitate the comprehension. But often, in modern talk as well as in the classical literature, the acting subject, if known as such from the context, retains its Nominative form. Especially the verba loquendi are apt to admit this slight irregularity.

31. Inflection of verbs. This is done in three different ways:

a) by changing the shape of the root. Such different shapes are, at most, four in number, which may be called, according to the tenses of our own grammar to which they correspond, the Present-, Perfect-, Future-, and Imperative-roots; e. g. of the Present-root གཏོང་བ་ ‚to give‘ the Perfect root is བཏང་, the Future-root གཏང་, the Imperative root ཐོང་; of འཚག་པ་ ‚to filter, bolt‘ respectively: བཙགས་ *tsag(s)* (Ü: *tsā*), བཙག་ *tsag*, ཚོག་ *tsog*. The Present root, which implies duration, is also occasionally used for the Imperfect (in the sense of the Latin and Greek languages) and Future tenses. It is obvious, from the above mentioned instances, that the inflection of the root consists partly in alterations of the prefixed letters (so, if the Perfect likes the prefixed བ, the Future will have ག or retain the བ), partly in adding a final ས་ (to the Perfect and Imperative), partly in changing the vowel (particularly in the Imperative). But also the consonants of the root itself are changed sometimes: so the aspirates are often converted in the Perfet and Future into their surds, besides other more irregular changes. Only a limited number of verbs, however, are possessed of all the four roots, some cannot assume more than three, some two, and a great many have only one. To make up in some measure for this deficiency:

b) some auxiliary verbs have been made available: for the Present tense ཨིན་, འདུག་, ལགས་ and others, all of which mean ‚to be‘ (§ 39); for the Perfect ཆར་, ཟིན་, སོང་; for the Future འགྱུར་, འོང་, and the substantive ཡི།

c) By adding various monosyllabic affixes, the Infinitive, Participles, and Gerunds are formed. These affixes as well as the auxiliary verbs are connected partly with the root, partly with the Infinitive, resp. its terminative, partly with the Participle.

Note. The spoken language, at least in WT, acknowledges even in four-rooted verbs seldom more than the Perfect root.

32. The Infinitive mood. The syllables པ་ *pa* or, after the final consonants ང་ ར་ ལ་ and vowels, བ་ *wa* are added to the root, whereby it assumes all the qualities and powers of a noun. In verbs of more roots than one, each of them can, of course, in this way be converted into a substantive, or, in other words, each tense has its Infinitive, except the Imperative. From one-rooted verbs the different Infinitives may be formed by the above mentioned auxiliaries: thus, the Inf. Perf., by adding ཡིན་པ་ to the Infinitive of the verb in question, or ཚར་བ་, ཟིན་པ་, ཐོང་བ་ to the root, and the Inf. Fut. by adding འགྱུར་བ་ to the Supine (terminative of the infinitive, 41. B) thus, མཐོང་བར་འགྱུར་བ་ visurum esse, visum iri.

Note. The spoken language uses, in WT almost exclusively, a termination pronounced *čas* in Turig and Balti, *čes, če* in Ladak, *če* in Lahoul etc., *ja* in Kunawar, *še* in Tsaṅ etc., the etymology of which is doubtful, as it is not to be found in any printed book. Lamas in Ladak and Lahoul spell it ཅེས་.

33. The Participle. 1. This is in the written language entirely like the Infinitive ཡིན་པ་ ‚being‘, གཏོང་བ་ ‚giving‘, བྱིང་བ་ ‚having given‘. — 2. Whether the meaning is active and passive, however, can only be inferred from the context, e. g. བྱིང་བའི་དངུལ་ is of course ‚the money given‘, but དངུལ་བྱིང་བའི་མི་ ‚the man having given, or, that has given, the money‘; the Tibetan participle means nothing but that the action or condition is connected in some way with a person or thing. But it is natural that in the present participle the active notion should be the more frequent one, as well as in the preterit the passive. — 3. In the instance of Intensive verbs (formed with བྱེད་པ་ 38. 1) the usage of scientific authors has strictly connected the active sense with those formed with བྱེད་, as གཏོང་བྱེད་ *toṅ-jed, toṅ-ǰĕ’*, instead of གཏོང་བར་བྱེད་པ་, doing give, giving, giver, and the passive to those with བྱ་, as གཏོང་བྱ་ *ton ja*, *ton ja* i. o. གཏོང་བར་བྱ་བ་ ,to be given' (dandus), བྱ་བ་དང་ བྱ་བ་མ་ཡིན་པ་སྟོན་པ་ ,to teach the things to be done and not to be done' (Thgy). — 4. In certain cases, especially with verbs that mean: to say, ask etc. the Participle is used before the words of the speech, where we should use the Imperfect: རྒྱལ་པོས་སྨྲས་པ་ ·· ,the king said . . .'.

Note. In the spoken language, of WT at least, the Participle is formed by མཁན་, in the active sense as well as the passive (whereas in books this syllable occurs only in the meaning of the performer of an action s. 12. 1.): དངུལ་བཏང་མཁན་གྱི་མི་ *ñul tan kan-ni mi* (s. 15, Note) ,the man giving the money', བཏང་མཁན་གྱི་དངུལ་ , the money given'. འདས་ལྐོག་གོན་ཆས་བཙོངས་མཁན་གྱི་བླ་མ་ ,the lama who brought a coat for sale the other day'. བུ་མོ་རྗེ་བཙུན་ ལ་སྒོ་ཁང་སྟོན་མཁན་དེ་ ,the girl who had shewn the door to his reverence' (Mil). The future participle is represented, just as in English, by the Infinitive (32, Note), so that ,the sheep to be killed', (in books གསོད་པར་བྱ་བའི་ལུག་ or གསོད་བྱའི་ལུག་) is expressed, in the most Western provinces, by: *sád cas-si lug*, Lad.: *sád-čes-si lug*, Lah. etc.: *sád čeï lug*, Tsan: *sö'-šẽ-kyi lug* གསོད་ཤེས་ཀྱི་ལུག་, and, most like the classical language, in Kun.: *sód jā̤ lug*.

34. The finite verb. 1. The principal verb of a sentence, which always closes it (48.) receives in written Tibetan in most cases a certain mark, by which the end of a period may be known. This is, in affirmative sentences, the vowel *o* (called by the grammarians: སྤྱར་སྤྱ་བ་), in interrogative ones the syllable *am*. Before both the closing consonant of the verb is repeated, or, if it ends with a vowel, འོ་ and འམ་ are written. The Perfect of the verbs ending in ན་ ར་ ལ་, which formerly had a ད་ as second final — ད་དྲག་ —, assume ཏོ་ and ཏམ་.— 2. These additional syllables are omitted *a*) in imperative sentences, *b*) in the latter member of a double question, *c*) when the question is expressed already by an interrogative pronoun or adverb, *d*) in coordinate members of a period, with exception of the last one, *e*) commonly, when the principal verb is the verb substantive ཡིན་, ཡོད་ etc. (40. 1.).

Examples. *a*) སོང་ ,go!', འདིར་ཤུ་ཤོག ,come here!'. — *b*) མཐོང་ངམ་མི་མཐོང་ ,do you see or not?' — *c*) དེ་ན་སུ་ཡོད ,who is there?', ནམ་བསླེབ་ ,when did (he, you etc.) arrive?'. — *d*) ཁང་པ་ཤིག ། མི་བསད། གྲོང་ཁྱེར་ཚང་མ་མེད་པར་བྱས་སོ ། ,the houses were destroyed, the men killed, the whole town annihilated'. — *e*) གཙང་པའི་བྱེ་མ་ལ་གསེར་ཡོད ། ,in the sand of the river is gold'.

Note. In conversation the *o* is generally omitted, and

the *m* of the interrogative termination dropped, so that merely the vowel *a* is heard, e. g. the question མཐོང་ངམ་ ‚do (you) see‘ and the answer མཐོང་ངོ་ ‚(I) see‘, are commonly spoken in WT: *ton-na? ton.*

35. Present Tenses. 1. Simple Present Tense. This is the simple root of the verb, which always will be found in the dictionary; in WT, as mentioned above, of verbs with more than one root, only the Perfect root is in use; if, therefore, stress is laid on the Present signification, recourse must be had te one of the following compositions, (s. 31. and Note). Thus, མཐོང་ ‚(I, thou, he etc.) see, seest etc.‘, གཏོང་ ‚(I etc.) give‘ through all persons; in the end of a sentence: མཐོང་ངོ་། གཏོང་ངོ་།

2. Compound Present Tenses. *a)* འདུག (s. 40, 1) is added to the root: མཐོང་འདུག ‚(I) see‘, བཏང་འདུག ‚(I) give‘. This is common in the dialect of WT especially. — *b)* The Participle connected with ཡིན, མཐོང་བ་ཡིན ‚(I) see‘. In WT this, of course, is changed to མཐོང་གཱན་ཡིན — *c)* One of the Gerunds (41, A) with ཡོད་ or འདུག, as མཐོང་སྟེ་ (or ནས་ or གི་ or ཞིང་), འདུག or ཡོད་ ‚(I) see, am seeing‘; it must, however, be remarked that both ways of expression, *b)* and *c)*, are not very frequent. — *d)* གིན་ཡོད་ or འདུག is the proper form for the compound

English present: མཐོང་གིན་འདུག ,(I) am seeing', འབྲི་གིན་
འདུག ,(I) am writing (just now)'.

36. Preterit Tenses. 1. Simple Preterit, Perfect or Aorist
Tense; this is the Perfect root: བྱིན་, at the close of the
sentence བྱིན་ནོ། ,gave, have given, was given'; in one-
rooted verbs it has, of course, the same form as the present:
མཐོང་(ངོ) ,saw, have, or was, seen'. This is the usual
narrative tense like the Greek Aorist or French Parfait
défini. — 2. Compound Preterit Tenses. — a) The root with
སོང་, བྱིན་སོང་ ,have given, gave, was given', མཐོང་སོང་
,have seen, saw, was seen'; rarely met with in books, but
in general use in the conversation of WT. In CT ཇུང་ *jun*
is used in a similar way: ཁྱིས་རྨུག་ཇུང་ ,the dog has bit'. —
b) The root with ཟིན་ (more in books), or ཆར་ (more in
common language), the true Perfect as the tense of accom-
plished action: བྱིན་ཟིན་, བྱིན་ཆར་ ,have given etc.', ,the
action of giving is past', མི་སོང་ཆར་ ,the man has already
left. — c) The Participle connected with ཡིན་ occurs more
frequently in the past sense than otherwise. Here, in the
common talk of WT, པ་ is used, even in those cases where
the books have བ་, ཡི་གེ་བཀལ་པ་ཡིན་ *yi-ge kál-pa yın*,
or, contracted, *kál-pen*, ,the letter has been sent off', in
books: བཀལ་བ་ཡིན་ (s. 11, Note), even སྐྲ་བྱངས་པ་ཡིན་

la *táns-pa yin*, *táns-pen*, ‚the wages have been paid‘ i. o.
བདང་བ་ཡིན་. — *d*) Gerunds in ཏེ (WT) or ནས་ (CT) with
ཡོད་ or འདུག (the same as 35. 2. *c*); also (in Ü Tsan and
later books) the mere Perfect root with ཡོད་, the ཏེ or
ནས་ being dropped: སོང་ཡོད་ ‚has gone‘.

37. Future Tenses.

1. Simple Future. The Future-root,
གཏོང་(ངོ་) ‚shall, will give, be given‘. — 2. Compound Future. *a*) The auxiliary verb འགྱུར་བ་ (to grow, become)
added to the Terminative case of the Infinitive: གཏོང་བར་
འགྱུར་(རོ་) ‚shall, will give, be given‘, མཐོང་བར་འགྱུར་(རོ་)
‚shall, will see, be seen‘. This is the most common, and,
together with the Simple Future and the Intensive (39.),
· · · བར་བྱའོ་, the only one in use with the early classical
authors in all cases where a special Future-root is wanted, and
even where this exists. It dissappears, however, gradually
from the literature of the later period, and is replaced by
the two following compositions. — *b*) རྒྱུ་ཡིན་ connected
with the root: མཐོང་རྒྱུ་ཡིན་ ‚shall, will see‘, གཏོང་རྒྱུ་ཡིན་
‚shall, will give‘ etc. (རྒྱུ་ is originally a substantive, meaning *material, cause, occasion*). — *c*) the root with འོང་ or
ཡོང་, སླེབ་ཡོང་ ‚will arrive‘, or, i. o. the root, the Term. Inf.,
སླེབ་པར་འོང་. — Both *b*) and *c*) are even now in common

use in CT, whereas in WT: — d) ཡིན་ connected with the root is the general form: མཐོང་ཡིན་ *toṅ yin*, vulg.: *tóṅin* ‚shall, will see‘, བདང་ཡིན་ *táṅin* ‚shall, will give‘, བཀལ་ཡིན་ *kállin* ‚will send‘, ཆ་ཡིན་ *ča yin*, *ča'in*, *čän* ‚will go‘. — e) In books the Participle with ཡིན་ (35. 2. *b*, 36. 2 *c*) occurs sometimes also as Future.

38. Imperative mood. 1. This is usually the shortest possible form of the verb, which often loses its prefixed letters, though in some instances a final ས་ is added. In many verbs with the vowel *a*, and in some with *e* these vowels are changed into *o*, besides other alterations of the consonants. Particularly often the surds or sonants of the other tense-roots are changed to their aspirates in the Imperative. Thus, སྦྱིན་ ‚give!‘, from གཏོང་བ་; ལྟོས་ Ld: *ltos*, CT: *ṭọ* ‚look!‘, from བལྟ་བ་; འཕེན་ ‚throw!‘, from འཕེན་པ་. In one-rooted verbs it is, of course, like the Present, but it can always be sufficiently distinguished by adding the particle ཅིག་ (ཞིག་ or ཤིག་, according to 13.). This is used in the classical literature indiscriminately in addressing the highest and the lowest persons (or, in other words, as well to command, as to pray), but according to the modern custom of CT only when addressing servants and inferior people. — 2. In for bidding, the Present-root is used with the negative particle མ་, མ་གཏོང་ ‚do not give!‘, མ་བྱ་ ‚do not look!', མ་འདེབས་ ‚do not throw!' — 3. In praying or wishing (Precative or Optative) either the same forms as under 1. are used, or the Imperatives of འབྱུང་བ་ ‚to come' or འོང་ ‚to come' (the latter, ཤོག་, of a quite different root) are connected with the Termin. Infin. མཐོང་བར་ གྱུར་ཅིག་ or ཤོག་ཅིག་ ‚may (I, you, he etc.) see!' — 4. In none of the three a person is indicated, but it is natural that in commanding and forbidding the subject will be the second, sometimes the third person; in the precative also the first person can be understood.

Note. The common language of WT, acknowledging only the Perfect-root, changes nothing but the vowel: བཏོང་ ‚give!' from བཏང་ཅེས་; ལྟོས་ ‚look!' from ལྟ་ཅེས་; བཏོབ་ ‚throw!' from བཏབ་ཅེས་ (Perf. of འདེབས་པ་). Instead of ཅིག་, which is not much used, བཏོང་ (give!) is often added to the roots of other verbs (s. 39), thus, བཏོན་བཏོང་ *ton ton* ‚take out!' from བཏོན་ཅེས་ (འདོན་པ་). Or the Imperative is paraphrased by དགོས་ *gos* (Ld). *gō, goi* ‚must', added to the root ot the verb: བསད་དགོས་ ‚must be killed'. — In CT the changing of the vowel seems to be usually omitted, but the ཅིག་ is more used. Here, also, the Perfect root is not so exclusively preferred.

39. Intensive verbs. 1. Very frequent in books is the

connection of the four-rooted verb བྱེད་པ་ (Pf. བྱས་, Fut. བྱ་, Imp. བྱོས་) ‚to do‘, elegantly བགྱིད་པ་ (Pf. བགྱིས་, Fut. བགྱི་, Imp. གྱིས་), respectfully མཛད་པ་ (Imp. མཛོད་) with the Term. Inf. of another verb, to intensify the action of the latter. By this means not only one-rooted verbs can be made to participate in the advantages of the four-rooted, as མཐོང་བར་བྱེད་ ‚see‘, མཐོང་བར་བྱས་ ‚saw‘, མཐོང་བར་བྱ་ ‚shall, will see‘, མཐོང་བར་བྱོས་ ‚see!‘, but also several other periphrastical phrases are gained for speaking more precisely than otherwise would be possible. The Future tense བྱ་(བའི་)་ serves, besides its proper notion of futurity, particularly to express the English auxiliaries ‚must, ought etc.‘: thus, བརྗོད་པར་མི་བྱའི་ ‚must not be uttered, ought not to be uttered‘, sometimes it may be translated by the Imperative mood. The spoken language, at least of WT, is devoid of this convenience, and possesses nothing of the kind except the above mentioned intensive form of the Imperative, formed by བདོང་ (s. 38., Note). — 2. Another class of intensive verbs are formed by connecting two synonymes, as འཇིགས་སྐྲག་པ་ ‚to be afraid‘, literally ‚to be fear-frightened‘, and other similar ones.

40. Substantive and Auxiliary Verbs. 1. To be *a*) ཡིན་ པ་, in elegant and respectful speech ལགས་པ་ *lag-pa*, Ü: *lā-pa* (the latter word never used in WT) is the mere means

of connecting the attribute with its subject, as: མི་འདི་ལ་ དྲགས་པ་ཡིན་ ,this man is a Ladakee‘, དེ་ཁྱེད་ལགས་སམ་ ,is it you, Sir?‘. Therefore the question སུ་ཡིན་ is to be understood ,who are you‘ or ,who is he‘ etc., the personal pronoun being often let to be guessed. — ཡིན་ itself is often omitted in daily life in WT as well as in poetry, e. g. ཨེ་ཁུར་ཅུ་མ་ ཕྱིན་ཏེ་ ,this load (is) very heavy‘ WT. Negatively: མ་ཡིན་, མིན་ vulg. མན་, resp. མ་ལགས་. — b) ཡོད་པ་ yod-pa, yö-pa, eleg. མཆིས་པ་ či-pa, resp. བཞུགས་པ་ žug(s)-pa, Ü: žū-pa, negat.: མེད་, མ་མཆིས་, མི་བཞུགས་ means ,to exist‘, or ,to be present‘, ,to be found at a place‘, therefore the question སུ་ཡོད་ is to be understood: ,Who is here? Who is there?‘ — ཡོད་ and བཞུགས་པ་ are in general use, མཆིས་ པ་ is seldom heard. When connected with the Dative of a substantive it replaces the English ,to have, to have got‘, as: ང་ལ་དངུལ་ཡོད་ ,I have money‘; ང་ལ་ཟུག་ཡོད་ ,I have pain‘. In this case the respectful term is not གཞུགས་པ་ but མངའ་བ་ ṅa-wa: རྒྱལ་པོ་ལ་སྙུན་མི་མངའ་འམ་ ,has not the King an indisposition?‘ i. e. ,is Your Majesty ill?‘. — c) འདུག་པ་ dug-pa (eleg. གདའ་བ་ is seldom heard), resp. བཞུགས་པ་, ,to be present, stay, be found at a place‘; negat.

མི་འདུག. Both འདུག་པ and ཡོད་པ can be used instead of ཡོད་པ, though not this instead of them. — d) རེད་པ rĕ"-pa = འདུག་པ, negat. མ་རེད in Spiti and CT, seldom in books. — e) མོད་པ mod-pa, mö"-pa has a somewhat emphatical sense: ‚to be (something) in a high degree‘, ‚to be (somehow) in plenty’. It occurs most frequently in the Gerund with ཀྱི (41.), when it frequently has the sense of ‚though‘, but never with a negative.— f) སྣང་བ nan-wa, originally ‚to appear, to be visible, extant‘, negat. མི་སྣང. Sometimes in books, and common in certain districts. — g) In books the concluding o (34.) is, moreover, fouud to represent the verb ‚to be‘ in all its meanings, and is capable of being connected with words of all classes besides verbs, e. g. དང་པོ་ནི ‚is the first‘ = དང་པོ་ཡིན. In a similar manner also the ཅིག of the Imperative (38.) implies the verb ‚to be‘. — h) The Preterit root for all these verbs is སོང son ‚was, has been‘, and besides also ‚has gone, become‘, which is its original meaning. — For the use of these verbs as auxiliaries s. 35. sq.

2. འགྱུར་བ originally ‚to be changed, turned into something‘ then ‚to become, to grow‘, auxiliary for the Future tense in the old classical language, as mentioned in 37. Since this can be considered as the intransitive or passive notion, opposite to བྱེད་པ ‚to make, render‘, the connection

of འགྱུར་བ་ with the Term. Inf. of another verb must, in many cases, be rendered by the passive voice in our languages. In WT the verb ཆ་ཆེས་ *ča-če* ‚to go‘ is used in the sense of ‚to become, to grow‘. The Perfect root for both is སོང་ ‚(went), grew, became, has become, is‘ (s. above). — In CT and later books འབྱུང་བ་ is used instead.

3. ‚must‘ is expressed by དགོས་པ་ ‚to be necessary‘ (s. 38. Note). In WT this is used in a very wide sense for any possible modification of the notion of necessity: ‚I must, should, want to, ought‘ and even ‚I will, wish, beg (for something)‘ is nothing but ང་ལ་དགོས་ ‚to me is necessary‘ which may be, in the last mentioned case, rendered somewhat more politely by adding ཞུ་ *žu* ‚pray!‘ ང་ལ་ཨ་ལུ་དགོས་ཞུ་ ‚I want potatoes, pray!‘ is as much to say as ‚Will you kindly give me some potatoes‘. In books and more refined language several other verbs are used in the same sense, viz. རིགས་པ་ ‚it is right to‘ (usually with the Genit. Infin.),

རུང་བ་ ‚it is meet, decent‘, འདོད་པ་ ‚to wish, desire‘, both with the Supine; དགའ་བ་ ‚to like‘ with the Dat. Inf. The popular substitute of the last, especially in use in WT, is འཕྲད་པ་, of similar meaning, added to the root.

41. Gerunds and Supines. We retain these terms, employed by former grammarians, but observe that they do not refer to the **form**, but to the **meaning**, as well as that Gerund is not to be understood in the same signification

as in Latin, but as the Gérondif of some French grammarians, or what Shakespeare calls Past conjunctive participle in Hindi. These forms are of the greatest importance
in Tibetan, being the only substitutes for most of those
subordinate clauses which we are accustomed to introduce
by conjunctions. They are formed by the two monosyllabic
appendices དེ་ (so after the closing consonants ན་ ར་ ལ་ ས་;
 དེ་ after ད, ཏེ་ after ག་ ང་ བ་ མ་ and vowels and ཅིང་ (ཞིང་
or ཤིང་ according to the same rule as ཅིག་ 13.), both of
which are added to the root, or by the terminations mentioned in 15. as composing the declension of nouns, which
are added partly to the root, partly to the Infinitive or
Participle.

A. Gerunds. All the following forms can be rendered
by the English Participle ending in *ing*, but the more ac-
curate distinctions must be expressed by various conjunctions.

1. ཏེ་ (དེ་ etc.), the most frequent of all these endings.
It is added to the Present-root as well as to the Perfect-root:
གཏོང་སྟེ་ ,giving‘, བཏང་སྟེ་ ,having given‘, and stands for all
clauses beginning with *when, as, since, after* etc. Also in
the spoken language of WT it is used most frequently. —
Examples: བུ་ག་ཆུས་ཁྱེར་ཏེ་ཤིད་ ,the child, having been carried away by the water, died‘; རྒྱལ་པོ་ཤི་སྟེ་རྒྱལ་སྲས་ཀྱིས་
རྒྱལ་ས་བཟུང་ངོ་ ,the king having died, the prince occupied

the throne (kings-place)'; ཆུ་ཆེན་པོ་ཞིག་དེ་རུ་ཡོད་དེ་འགྲུལ་མི་ཐུབ་བོ་ ,as there is a great water, we cannot go'.

2. ཅིང་ (ཤིང་ etc.), of a similar sense, chiefly used for smaller clauses within a large one; མི་དགའ་ཞིང་ཁྲོས་ཏེ་ ,when, being displeased, he became angry', or ,growing displeased and angry'. Often it denotes two actions going on at the same time, or two states of a thing existing together, and then can only be translated by ,and', thus, མཐའ་མེད་ཅིང་མུ་མེད་ ,without end and boundary'; ཤ་ལ་ཟ་ཞིང་ཁྲག་ལ་འཐུང་བ་ ,to eat flesh and drink blood'*). It stands also in a causal sense: ,by doing etc.', as: ཉ་བཤོར་ཞིང་འཚོ་འོ་ ,(we) live by catching fish'. These two (1. and 2.) can also, like the closing *o*, as mentioned in 40. 1. *g*, be added to every class of words, in the sense of *being*: ཁྱོད་རིགས་ཆེ་ཞིང་མཐོ་བ་སྟེ་ ,as you are high (-born), being of a great family'. In conversation, ཅིང་ is scarcely ever heard.

3. ནས་ (from, or after, doing something) in temporal clauses with ,after, when, as'; practically it is very much like ཏེ་, and often alternating with it. In most cases, in speaking always, it is added to the root, seldom to the infi-

---

*) The objects of ཟ་བ་ and འཐུང་བ་ often assume the dative-sign, cf. English ,to feed on'.

nitive.— *Examples.* ནུམ་ལངས་ནས་སོང་ ,when the night had risen (viz. at daybreak) he went'; ལང་ནས་སོང་ ,after you will have risen, go!' དེ་མཐོང་ནས་སྐད་ཕྱུང་སྟེ་ངུས་སོ ,when I saw that, raising clamour, I wept'.

4. ན ,in (doing something)' again for clauses with ,since, when, as', but in most cases by far for ,if' and con-ditional ,when': འགྲོ་ན ,if, or, when (I) go, or went'; ཤི་ ཚར་ན ,when, after (he) has died', ,if he is already dead'; ཤི་ན ,if (he) die, should die', ,if (he) died', ,when (he) dies'; བྱེད་ན ,if .. do, did'; བྱ་ན ,if .. were to do'. It is added to the root, seldom to the infinitive, and as common in talking as in books.

5. ལ is of more various use. When added to the root, it is very much like ཅིང་, which it replaces in the conver-sational language of CT (where the first example of 2. would be, མ་དགའ་ལ་བྲོས་ཏེ), but does not occur so often except in imperative or precative sentences, when it is added to the Imperative root of the subordinate verb, just like other gerunds: སོང་ལ་ལྟོས ,going look!', ,go and look!' བོང་ལ་ སོང་ ,rise and go!'. This particle, like the above-mentioned, implies the verb ,to be', especially when added to adjec-tives denoting a personal quality. མི་སྡུག་ལ་ཕྱུང་དུ་ཡིན་ཏེ ,being ugly and short'; དབྱིབས་ལེགས་ཤིང་ལྡ་ན་སྡུག་ལ་མཛེས

ལ་ ,pretty, being of a good figure and nice to behold'. When added to the Infinitive, it denotes: *a*) of course, the real Dative, or the usual meanings of the postposition ལ་ with a substantive; thus, གསོད་པ་ལ་དགའ་བ་ ,to rejoice at killing, be fond of killing'. *b*) nearly the same as དེ་ or ,as' in English, e. g. ལམ་གྱི་བར་དུ་ལྷ་རྟེན་ཞིག་ཡོད་པ་ལ་ཞིང་ད་ལས་ བབ་བོ་ ,as there was an idol-shrine in the middle of the way, (she) alighted from (her) chariot'; རྒྱལ་པོ་ཉིན་རེ་བཞིན་ དུ་རེར་ཁྲུས་བྱེད་དུ་འགྲོ་བ་ལ་ ,as the king went there daily to bathe'; འཇིག་རྟེན་གྱི་ནང་ན་མི་འོང་བ་ལ་འདི་དུ་འོང་བ་ཅི་ཡིན་ ,as (it) does not occur in the (whole) world, what is (its) oc-curring here, or, how is it that is occurs here?'. Finally, in the language of common life ལ་ is added to the repeated root in order to express the English ,while, whilst': ངས་ ཤ་གཏུབ་གཏུབ་ལ་ཁྱོད་ཀྱིས་ཤིང་ཁྱོང་ *n̄ā śa tub-túb-la ǩyód-dĭ* (15., Note) *śiṅ ǩyoṅ* WT, or ཁྱོད་ཀྱིས་ཤིང་བགུར་ཤོག *ǩyö̆-kyĭ śiṅ kur-śog* CT ,while I am cutting the meat into pieces, bring you (some) wood'.

      6. ལས་ added only to the Infinitive, literally ,out of (the doing)'. This may mean *a*) ,after', ཉལ་བ་ལས་ལང་ བ་ ,to rise from lying, after having lain'; དུར་ན་ཞག་གསུམ་ འདུག་པ་ལས་དར་ནས་བྱུང་ ,after having been three days in

the grave (I) came out of the grave'. — b) ‚while‘, in which case the root of the verb may be repeated, as: སོང་ སོང་བ་ལས་བྱུས་ཙེ་ཞིག་དང་ཕྲད་དོ ‚out of my walking i.e. when walking along, (I) met with a brahman‘; ང་ ཤ་གཙུབ་གཙུབ་ པ་ལས་ཁྱོད་ཀྱིས་ཞིང་བགྱུར་ཏེ་འོག (the above mentioned example (s. ལ་) translated into classical language); c) also the English ‚being about to‘ is, in books, often expressed by this Gerund: ཞེད་དུ་སོང་བ་ལས་སྒོ་བཅད་དོ ‚when (I) was about to enter, the door was shut‘; ཤི་བ་ལས་ཕྱིར་སོས་པར གྱུར་དོ ‚when (I) was going to die, (I) was restored to life again‘. Which of the three is the real meaning, will in most cases be clear from circumstances. This gerund is not used in talking, at least in WT.

7. ཀྱིས་ (གྱིས་ etc.) or ཀྱི་ (གྱི་ etc.), or the Instrumental and Genitive cases of the root, mean a) ‚by doing something‘ or ‚because‘, e.g. དགོས་ཀྱིས་འདོང་དོ ‚we come (here), because it is necessary‘. ཁོ་མོས་གྲོགས་བྱ་ཡིས་སྙིང་མ་ཆུང ཞིག ‚since I am resolved to help you, do not be depressed!‘ This, originally, is a function of the Instrumental only, but in later times the other cases also are used in this meaning. — b) more frequently they are used adversatively, ‚though‘, especially when connected with མོད་ (40. 1. e), ཅེས་སྨྲས་མོད་ཀྱིས་ཅེས་ཡིད་ཆེས་པར་འགྱུར ‚though (you) did

say so, by what shall (I) believe (it)?' In other cases
it may be left untranslated when the next sentence will
commence with ‚but': ཟས་བཟང་པོ་མི་འདོད་ཀྱིས་ཟས་ཐ་མལ་
པ་ཟོས་སོ་ ,not liking delicate food, he ate vulgar food' or
‚he did not like d. f., but preferred v. f.'. This Gerund is
scarcely used in talking, at least in WT.

8. པས་ (བས་), the Instrumental of the Infinitive, ‚by
(doing something)' is, of course, the proper expression for
‚because', but also very often used indiscriminately for དེ་
or ནས་ only for the sake of varying the mode of speaking:
ཤིན་ཏུ་དཀའ་བ་ཡིན་པས་ ,because it is very difficult'; བལྟས་
པས་ ,when (he) looked'.

9. Also གིན་ the proper use of which has been shewn
above (35. 2. d.) must be mentioned once more as it occurs
in a similar sense to ཅིང་, སྨོན་ལམ་འདེབས་གིན་སོང་ཞིག
,walk on praying (preces faciendo)!'; བྲང་བརྡུང་གིན་དུས་པས་
,beating (her own) breast and weeping'.

B. Supines. They are expressed simply by the Terminative Case of the Infinitive or of the Root, མཐོང་བར་
or ཐོང་དུ་ ,to see'. In many instances the use of either is
optional, in others one is preferred. Their use is: with
adjectives like the Latin supine in u, e.g. བསླབ་ཏུ་དཀའ་བ་
,difficult to learn'; with verbs expressing ,to go, to send' etc.,

also ‚to pray‘ etc. like that in *um*: ལེན་དུ་སོང་ ‚go to fetch‘, གནང་དུ་གསོལ་ ‚(I) beg (you) to permit, — for permission‘. In these cases the root is most common, but the Inf. བསྒྲུབ་ པར་, or གནང་བར་, ལེན་པར་ may also be used. 2. Another use of the Supine is *a*) with verbs of sensation and, less frequently, with those of declaration, where we use sentences with ‚that‘ or the Participle or Infinitive: མ་འོང་བར་མཐོང་ ནས་ ‚seeing (his) mother coming‘ (instead of which, however, འོང་བ་ may be said as well); ··· བའི་དུས་ལ་བབ་པར་ ་ཤེས་ནས་ ‚knowing that the time of . . . ing had arrived‘ (lit: ‚that it had come down to the time‘); རྒྱལ་པོ་འི་བུ་ཡིན་ པར་དྲན་ནས་ ‚remembering him to be the kings son‘ or ‚that he was . . .‘. — *b*) in an adverbial sense, when we say ‚so that‘, especially in negative sentences, ‚so that not‘ ‚without . . . ing‘, སུས་ཀྱང་མ་ཚོར་བར་ ‚so that nobody may (did) perceive it‘, or ‚without anybody perceiving it.‘

Note 1. The modern language of WT uses in the first instance (B. 1.) either the simple Infinitive, བསྒྲུབ་ཆེས་ཁག་ པོ་ (or དགག་པོ་), or the same with ལ་, བསྒྲུབ་ཆེས་ལ་ཁག་ པོ་, or with ཕྱི་ལ་ (for the ཕྱིར་ of the books s. 7.2.), བསྒྲུབ་ ཆེས་ཕྱི་ལ་ཁག་པོ་; in the second either the same forms, or a particular one, which consists in repeating the final consonant of the root with the vowel *a*, to which also ལ་ may be added: thus, ལེན་ན་སོང་, ཁྱོད་རང་ལ་ཐུག་ག་ལ་ཡོངས་སོང་ ,(I) have come to meet you'; in the third, the direct Imperative adding ཅུ་ for the sake of civility, དགོངས་ཅུ་ ,pray permit!'

In the case of B. 2., instead of མ་འོང་བར་མཐོང་ནས་; the expression in common use will be ཨ་མ་ཡོང་ or ཡོང་ ང་མཐོང་ནས་; instead of སུས་ཀྱང་མ་ཚོར་བར་, either the same form, མ་ཚོར་ར་, or the Gerund, མ་ཚོར་ཏེ་. — In CT those examples would respectively, stand thus, བསླབ་ཏུ་ or བསླབ་ བ་ or བསླབ་པའི་དོན་ཏུ་དགག་པོ་ *láb-tu, láb-ba* (sounding almost *lă-wa*), *láb-pa ḍon-ḍu kag-po*; in the third instance a peculiar word, ,*rog*', is used, which is said to be originally the same as གྲོགས་ (རོགས་) ,friend,assistant',and serves now as the respectful substitute of ཅིག་, Particle of the Imperative, གནང་རོག་ ,pray permit!', སྤྱེར་རོག་ ,pray give!' Instead of མ་ཚོར་ར་ etc. the most usual form in CT will be the simple Participle, མ་ཤེས་པ་.

Note 2. All the forms, of course, where པ་ or བ་ are met with might in certain cases belong to the Participle, and not to the Infinitive.

Note 3. The reader will have missed any mention of tenses of the class of Pluperfect, Past Future etc., and,

indeed, there exists no form of the kind, and they can only
be rendered by a Gerund, e.g. ཨི་གི་བྱིས་ཏེན་ནས་བཀལ་སོང་
,when (he) had written the letter, (he) sent (it) off'; ཨི་གི་
བྱིས་ཏེན་ནས་བཀལ་བར་འགྱུར (WT: བཀལ་ཡིན་, CT: བཀལ་
ཀྱུ་ཡིན་) ,when (he) shall have written the letter, (he) will
sent (it) off'. Neither have the Conditional or Subjunctive
any special form. Thus, e.g., འདི་མ་བྱས་ན་མི་འཚོ་ཏོ ,if
we did not do that, we could not live (i.e. we cannot earn
our sustenance in any other manner); ཅིའི་ཕྱིར་ཁྱོད་ཟེར་བ་ནི་མི་
ཉན ,why should not I hear (grant) what you say (your
wish)?'; བཤད་མ་བཀྲོལ་ཞིང་དགས་མ་མཐོང་ན་མི་རྟོགས་པར་འདུག
,if (you) had not explained it, and (we) had not seen the
signs, we would not have understood it'; མིས་མི་རྙེད་པས་
སྤྲུལ་པ་ཅིག་བཏག་དགོས ,as a man would not find it, I must
send an emanation'; vulg., WT, ཨི་ཐུག་ཐག་རིང་མ་ཡིན་ན་
འདི་རུར་འགྲོ་དུ་ཡོང་ཡིན ,if the distance was not so great,
they would come to me (visit me)'. Here may be added,
that also the intention of, or attempt at, doing something
is expressed by the simple verb: thus, བདག་གིས་བཀག
ཡང་མ་བཏུབ་ཀྱིས ,though I did try to hinder him, I could
not'; བདག་གི་ཉི་གནས་ཆུར་མཆོངས་པ་མཐོང་ནས། ཆུར་མ་ཕྱིན
པར་རྟ་འཕུལ་གྱི་མཐུས་སྲངས་སོ ,as he saw his own disciple

on the point of springing into the water (and that he had
sprung off the bank), he held him back by the force of his
magic, so that he did not touch the water' (s. 41. B. 2. b.).
Especially the gerunds in ལས་ (41. A. 6.) have often this

meaning: བདག་སྲོག་དང་བྲལ་བ་ལས་སྲོག་གི་སྐྱབས་བྱས་སོ་
,when I was about to be parted from life, he saved it';

སྤུལ་ཁྲིས་ནས་གདུག་པ་སྤྱུང་བ་ལས་ཡང་འདི་སྐྱམས་བསམས་སོ་
,the snake, having become angry, though she intended (or:
had at first int.) to let out her poison, reflected thus'. As
will be seen from these examples, the action, in such cases,
is thought to have begun in fact.

A Survey of the principal forms of the Finite Verb.

Present:

གཏོང་,   W བདང་འདུག give

མཐོང་བ་ཡིན   མཐོང་གཏན་ཡིན I see   intens. མཐོང་བར་བྱེད

C མཐོང་སྟེ་འདུག (or ཡོད་)

W མཐོང་གིན་འདུག (or ཡོད་); C མཐོང་གི་འདུག

I am seeing

Perfect:

བདང་   W བདང་སོང་ gave, have given

མཐོང་   C མཐོང་བྱུང་ saw, W སོང་སྟེ་ཡོད་   C སོང་ཡོད་

went   went

བདང་བྱིན་   བདང་ཚར་ I have given, intens. མཐོང་བར་བྱས་

བདངས་པ་ཡིན་ has been given

Future:

གདང་   W བདང་ཡིན་ shall, will give

མཐོང་བར་འགྱུར་ C མཐོང་རྒྱུ་ཡིན་   intens. མཐོང་བར་བུ་

shall, will see

སླེབ་ཡོང་, སླེབ་པར་འོང་ will arrive

Imperative:

སྟོང་ W བཏོང་ give!   བཏོན་བཏོང་ take out!   བསད་དགོས་ kill!

མཐོང་ཅིག་ see!   intens. མཐོང་བར་བྱོས་

negat. མ་གཏོང་   མ་བཏང་ do not give!   མཐོང་བར་མ་བྱེད་

Chapter VII.

The Adverb.

42. We may distinguish three classes of adverbs:
1. Primitive adverbs. 2. Adverbs formed from Adjectives.
3. Adverbs formed from Substantives or Pronouns.

1. Very few Primitive Adverbs occur; the most usual
are: ད་ ,now‘, ནམ་ ,when‘, སང་ (books and CT) or ཐོ་ར་
(WT) ,to morrow‘, and a few similar ones; ཡང་ ,again‘,
and the two negatives མི་ and མ་, the latter of which is
used in prohibitive sentences, and with a past tense, as
མི་གཏོང་ ,(I) do not give‘, མི་བཏང་ ,(I) shall not give‘, but:
མ་བཏང་ ,did not give‘, མ་གཏོང་ (WT: མ་བཏང་) ,do not

give!' The verbs ཡིན་, ལྟགས་, མཆིས་, རེད་ have always
མ་ instead of མི་ before them (40.). Another particle of
this kind, of a merely formal value, is ནི་, which is added
to any word or group of words in order to single it out
and distinctly separate it from everything that follows. It
is, therefore, often very useful in lessening the great in-
distinctness of the language, especially so when separating
the subject from the attribute: མི་དེ་ནི་ལ་དྭགས་པ་ཡིན་ ,that
man is a Ladakee'. (There is scarcely an adequate word
to be found in our modern languages, but the Greek γε,
or μεν— δε—, are very similar.) In talking it is seldom
heard, and, when used, in WT pronounced: ནིང་.

2. Adverbs may be formed from any Adjective by
putting it in the Terminative case. བཟང་པོ་ ,good', བཟང་པོར་
,well'; རབ་ ,principal', རབ་ཏུ་ ,principal, very'; དྲག་
པོ་ ,violent', དྲག་པོར་ or དྲག་ཏུ་ ,violently'.

3. Nearly all the local Adverbs are formed from
Substantives or Pronouns with some local Postposition:
གོང་ ,the place (space) above, upper part', གོང་ན་ ,above',
གོང་ཏུ་ ,upwards'. གོང་ནས་ ,from above (downwards)'; འདི་
,this', འདི་ན་ ,in this, here', འདི་རུ་, འདིར་ ,hither, here'
(cf. 15.), འདི་ནས་ ,hence'; དེ་ ,that', དེ་ན་ ,there', དེ་རུ་, དེར་
,thither, there', དེ་ནས་ ,from there, thence, then, after that'.

Note. In talking the simple adjective is used, mostly, instead of its adverb (2. class): མགྱོགས་པ་ for — པར་ ‚quickly, soon‘.

Chapter VIII.

The Postposition.

43. There are two kinds of Postpositions: 1. Simple Postpositions. These are the same that we know already as forming the cases (15). 2. Compound Postpositions, formed in the manner of local Adverbs (42. 3), with which they are, indeed, with a few exceptions, identical.

1. Simple Postpositions. These are: ལ་ (the affix of the Dative), ན་ (Locative), ནས་ and ལས་ (Ablative), ཏུ་, ར་, སུ་, དུ་, རུ་ (Terminative).

Their use will be best seen in the following examples:

༎ ལ་ ༎

ཕན་རྡིལ་མེ་ལ་བོར་ WT, རྫངས་མེ་ལ་བཞག་ (inst. of ཞོག 38, Note) CT ‚put the degchi on the fire!‘.

བོང་བུ་ས་ལ་འགྲེའོ་, vulg: འགྲེ་འདུག, Tsang: བོང་གུ་ས་ལ་ འགྲེ་གིས་ ‚the ass rolls himself on the ground‘.

རྟ་ལ་ཞོན་ཏེ་ (or ནས་) འགྲོ་ ‚having mounted on the horse (he) goes‘, or ‚(he) goes on horseback‘.

བུ་ནས་གཏན་ལ་འཕྱུར་རོ་, vulg (WT): ཅི་པ་ (corrupted from

མཆིལ་པ༻ ནམ་མཁའ་ལ་འཕུར་འདུག, CT: བྱ་ནམ་མཁའ་ ལ་འཕིར་གིས་འདུག ,the bird flies in the sky'.

མཚན་ལ་ཆ་ཡིན་ WT, ནམ་ལ་འགྲོ་རྒྱུ་ཡིན་ CT ,(we) shall set out at night'.

དེ་ལ་ཤིན་ཏུ་དགའ་སྟེ་ (books and CT), དེ་ལ་མང་པོ་འཕང་དེ་ WT ,being very glad at this'.

སྨན་ལ་མཁས་པ་ ,skilful in medicine'.

ཆང་ལ་བོས་སོ, vulg: བོས་སོང་ ,invited him to beer'.

མགོ་ལ་ཟུག་རག་ག WT, འདུག་གམ CT ,is (there) ache in (your) head', ,have you head-ache?'

‖ ན་, དུ་ etc. ‖

ཁྱིམ་ན་ (or དུ) ཡོད་, vulg: ཁང་པ་ལ་ (or རུ) ཡོད་ ,(he) is in the house, at home'.

ཁྱིམ་དུ་སོང་, vulg: ཁང་པ་རུ་ (or ལ) སོང་ ,go into the house, home!'.

དུས་ཅིག་ན་, vulg: ཞག་ཅིག ,at a (certain) time, once'.

ད་སྟེ་ཞག་བདུན་ན་ (books) ,from to-day in (after) seven days'.

མས་བུ་པང་པར་ཁྱེར་རོ; WT: ཨ་མས་བུ་ཚ་པང་ལ་ཁྱར་ཁྱིར; CT: ཨ་མས་བུ་པང་གར་ཁྱར་སོང་ ,the mother carried the son in (her) arms'.

དེའི་དུས་སུ་, vulg: དེ་དུས་ ,at that time'.

ལོ་བདུན་དུ་ (books, for vulg. see Compound adv.) ,for seven years'.

མི་དེ་རྒྱལ་པོར་བཅུག་གོ (or བསྐོས་སོ་), W: རྒྱལ་པོ་ལ་བདག ,(they) made (or selected, raised) that man to (be) king'.

འོ་བུད་སྲས་སུ་བཅུག་གོ, CT: འཁྲི་བུད་ (or ཚ་ལག་) སྲས་ལ་ བཅུག་ ,(they) made (their) luggage into a pillow, used it as a pillow'.

གང་དུ་ (or ག་རུ་) འགྲོ, WT: ག་རུ་ཆ་མ་ཁན་ (s. 35. 2. *b*, ཡིན་ omitted, 40. 1. *a*), CT: ག་ལ་འགྲོ་གིས་ཡིན་ (པ་ or བས་, provincial irregularities 35.2.*c*) ,where are (you) going?'

ང་ཏི་ནོར་ (or ཁོག་སར་ལ་) འགྱལ་འདུག (vulg.) ,I am going to Tino (or K'oksar)'.

|| ནས་ ||

ཟླ་བ་བརྒྱད་ནས་ ,after eight months'.

ཟླ་བ་བརྒྱད་པ་ནས་ ,from (after) the eighth month'.

ཐོག་མ་ནས་ (books and CT), WT: མགོ་མ་ནས་ ,from the beginning'.

|| ལས་ ||

དཀར་ཁང་ལས་ ,from the window, through the window'.

འཁོར་བ་ལས་འགྲོལ་བ་, vulg: ··· ནས་བསྒྲལ་བ་ , to deliver from the circulation (transmigration)'.

པ་གུ་ལས་ཁང་པ་རྩིག་པ་, WT: ནས་, Tsang: པ་གུའི་ནང་རྩིག་ པ་ ,to build a house out of brick (Ts: a house of brick)'.

མདོ་ཟ་མ་ཏོག་ལས་ ,from the sūtra Zamatog'.

སློབ་མ་ལས་གཅིག (vulg: སློབ་མའི་ནང་ནས་གཅིག) ‚one of
(from among) the pupils‘.

ཀུན་ལས་མཁས་པ་ (books and CT), WT: ཚང་མའི་རང་མཁས་
པ་ ‚wiser than all, the wisest, most skilful of all‘.

གཉིས་ལས་མ་ལྷུས་སོ་ ‚more than two are not left‘.

ང་ལས་མི་འདུག ‚more than myself are not‘.

Besides these རང་ ‚with‘ is to be mentioned as Simple
Postposition : thus , ཁྱིའུ་དང་སྨྲས་ཏེ་ , WT: ཕྲུག་གོང་དང་
ལབ་སྟེ་ ‚speaking (conversing) with the youth‘; ང་དང་ ‚with
me‘, or, in fuller form, ང་དང་ལྷན་གཅིག་ཏུ་, ང་དང་བཅས་སུ་
vulg: ང་དང་མཉམ་པོ་ ‚together with me‘. In WT it is even
used for the instrumental when the real instrument (tool)
of an action is meant, e. g. རྒྱལ་པོས་བློན་པོ་རལ་གྲིས་བསད་
so in books, but WT: རལ་གྲི་དང་བསད་ ‚the king killed the
minister with the sword‘. It is, moreover, added to many
Adjectives and Verbs, when we use the Accusative or Dative or other Prepositions, e.g. དེ་དང་འདྲ་བ་ ‚like (with)
that, similar to that‘. With an Infinitive it denotes the
synchronism of the action with another one, ཉི་མ་འཆར་བ་
དང་ ‚with the sun rising, at sunrise‘; གཉིད་སོང་བ་དང་ ‚with
(on) their going to sleep, when they went to sleep‘;
ཅེས་སྨྲས་པ་དང་ཁྱིམ་དུ་སོང་ ‚(with) saying so he went home‘
or also ‚he said so, and went home‘. Often it is found with

an Imperative, without any perceptible signification, if it
is not to be regarded as a substitute for ཅིག་ (38): ད་ཟོ་དང་
‚now eat!‘ For its use as a conjunction see the next chapter.

2. Compound Postpositions. These may con-
veniently be grouped in two classes: *a*) Local Compound
Postpositions, which are virtually the same as the Local
Adverbs specified in 42.3.: thus, ནང་ན་ ‚in (the midst of)‘,

ནང་དུ་ ‚into‘ also ‚in‘, ནང་ནས་ ‚from, out of‘. The most usual
ones will be seen in the following examples:

རྫིང་གི་ནང་ན་ (or དུ་) ཁྲུས་བྱེད་པ་ ‚to bathe in a pond‘.

ཆུའི་ནང་དུ་ཞུགས་ ‚he entered into the water‘ (both in books
and common talk).

ལྷའི་ནང་ན་གཙོ་བོ་ ‚the lord among the gods‘.

ཁང་པའི་ནང་ནས་འཐོན་ (or འབྱུང་) vulg. ‚(he) comes (emerges)
out of the house‘.

སྒོའི་གོང་དུ་ (or ན་, or ལ་) ‚above the door‘ (books and
vulg., but more usual in WT: སྒོ་ལྟག་, CT སྒོ་ཐོད་).

ཡབ་ཀྱི་གོང་དུ་འདས་ vulg.: ཡབ་ཀྱི་སྔན་ལ་ (or སྔ་ལ་), CT
also གདོང་ལ་ ‚he died before his father‘.

པདྨའི་སྟེང་དུ་ (or ན་, or ཐོག་དུ་, or ཁ་རུ) བཞུགས་པ་, vulg., in
WT: ཁ་ཐོག་ལ་ (ཁ་ཐོད་ལ་), CT: དཀྱིང་ལ་ ‚to sit on a
lotus-flower‘.

སྒོའི་འགྲམ་དུ་ (or ལ་, or ན་) (books and talk) ,beside,near the door'.

ཤིང་གི་དྲུང་དུ་, vulg.: མདུན་ལ་, རྩ་ན་, རྩར་ ,under a tree' (literally: ,in front, by the side, of a tree').

ཁལ་ཆེ་བའི་དྲུང་དུ་ (མདུན་དུ་) འཁྲིད་པ་ ,to take before the judge'.

ཟླ་བ་བརྒྱད་ཀྱི་རྗེས་ལ་ CT, རྟིང་ལ་ WT ,after eight months'.

ཟླ་བ་གཉིས་ཀྱི་སྔོན་ལ་ (or སྔན་ལ་) vulg. ,before two months, two months ago'.

སའི་འོག་ཏུ་གཏེར་སྦེད་པ་ books and CT, WT: སའི་འོག་ལ་ གཏེར་སྦ་བ་ ,to hide a treasure below the ground'.

སའི་འོག་ནས་འབྱུང་བ་ CT, WT: སའི་ཡོག་ནས་འཕྲོན་པ་ ,to emerge, come out, from below the ground'.

ཆུའི་ཕ་རོལ་ན་ books and CT, in CT also: ཕར་ཕྱོགས་པ་, WT: ཕར་ཁ་ལ་, ཕར་ཚེས་ལ་ ,beyond the water, river'.

ཆུའི་ཚུ་རོལ་ན་ books and CT, WT: ཚུར་ཁ་ལ་ ,on this side of the water'.

ཞག་གསུམ་དུ་ (or ནས་) ཐང་དེའི་ཕ་རོལ་དུ་ཕྱིན་པར་འགྱུར་རོ་,CT: ཕ་རོལ་དུ་སྙེབ་འོང་, WT: ཕར་ཁ་ལ་སྙེབ་ཡིན་ ,in (after) three days he will arrive beyond this plain, will have crossed it'.

ཁང་པའི་ཕྱོགས་བཞི་རུ་ ,in the four regions of the house, roundabout'.

ཡུལ་དེའི་ཕྱོགས་ལ་སོང་ ,go in the direction of, towards, that village‘.

ལོ་བདུན་གྱི་བར་དུ, CT: ལོ་བདུན་ཕྲག་(པ་), WT: ˮ ཚུག་པ་ ,for seven years‘.

འདི་ནས་དེའི་བར་དུ, CT: འདི་ནས་དེ་ཕྲག་པ་, WT: ཨི་ནས་ཨ་ ཚུག་པ་ ,from this to that‘.

ང་ཞུང་དེ་རུ་ཚ་ཆེས་ཚུག་པ་ WT, ,till I go to Kullu‘.

b) General Compound Postpositions, expressive of the general relations of things and persons. They are formed in the same manner as the Local ones, from substantives, adjectives, and even verbs. Their use may be learned from the following examples:

ངའི་ཕྱིར་(དུ་) or དོན་དུ་ books and CT, WT: ངའི་པོ་ལ་ ,for me, in my behalf, for my sake, on my account‘.

ནད་དེ་ནི་ཅིའི་ཕྱིར་བྱུང་, WT: ཅིའི་པེ་ལ་ཡོངས་, CT: གང་གི་དོན་ དུ་བྱུང་ ,for what reason has that illness come? what is the cause of etc.?‘.

སེམས་ཅན་ཐམས་ཅད་ཀྱི་དོན་དུ་ ,in behalf of all living beings‘.

ཤིང་གི་ཚབ་ལ་རྡོ་ (WT: རྡོབ་) བྱིང་ ,give (apply) stone instead of wood‘.

བཞིན་དུ་ ,according to, like, as‘ — རྒྱལ་པོ་འི་བཀའ་བཞིན་ དུ་བྱས་ཏེ་ ,doing according to the word of the king‘; དེ་

བཞིན་དུ་ ‚according to that, like that, thus, so‘; སྔ་མ་བཞིན་དུ་ ‚as formerly, as before‘; instead of it the dialect of WT uses ནང་ལྟར་, generally with the Genitive, thus the last example there would be: སྔན་མའི་ནང་ལྟར་.

ལྟར་ ‚like‘, རི་ལྟར་ ‚like a hill‘; འདི་ལྟར་, དེ་ལྟར་ ‚like this, like that, thus, so, ཅི་ལྟར་, CT: གང་ལྟར་ ‚like what? how? in what manner?‘.

In the dialect of WT མཚོགས་ or མཚོགས་སེ་ is used instead (which is a corruption of མཚུངས་, occurring in books with the same meaning): thus, རི་མཚོགས་སེ་ ‚like a hill‘; འདི་མཚོགས་, དེ་མཚོགས་ ‚thus‘; or ཟུག་ (properly ཚུག་), ཨི་ཟུག་, ཨ་ཟུག་ ‚thus‘, ག་ཟུག་ ‚how?‘.

Chapter IX.
The Conjunction.

44. The written language possesses very few, the spoken still fewer, Conjunctions, most of which are coordinative. The common word for ‚and‘ is དང་ which we have seen above in the sense of ‚with‘, གསེར་དང་། དངུལ་དང་། ལྕགས་ལ་སོགས་པ་ ‚gold and silver and iron and collection (i. e. and so on)‘, though the position of the *šad* (10:) after the word དང་ shows that it is always considered as belonging to the preceding member of the sentence, similar, in this respect, to the Latin ‚que‘; nor can it in any case begin a sentence. Very seldom, and only in later literature, it appears as combining two verbs, if not, indeed, the root ought to be regarded there as abbreviation for the infinitive. Further: ཡང་ ‚also, too‘. When belonging to a single word or notion it is put after it in an enclitical way like ‚quoque‘ in Latin. It is changed according to the termination of the preceding word, into ཀྱང་ after ག་ ད་ བ་ ས་*), into འང་ often after vowels (cf. 6). Thus: བུ་ཞིག་ ཀྱང་ཁྲིད་དེ་ ‚taking also a son (with him)‘. When repeated, it has the signification of Latin ‚et— et—‘, མ་ཡང་ཤི། བུ་ ཡང་ཤིའོ ॥ ‚both mother and son died‘. Often, especially in negative sentences, it means ‚even‘, གཅིག་ཀྱང་མ་རྙེད་དོ་ ‚even one (they) did not find — not even one‘. This is the only means for expressing ‚none, no, nothing‘, མི་སུ་ (or གང་) ཡང་མ་འོངས་ (resp. ཡོངས་) ‚nobody came‘; དེ་ན་ཅི་ ཡང་ (ཅིའང་, or ཅང་) མེད་ ‚there is nothing‘ (cf. 29). When combined with verbs, བཙལ་ཡང་མ་རྙེད་དོ་ ‚even searching (they) did not find‘, it serves as another expression for ‚though‘ or also ‚but‘ (s. 41. A. 7. b): thus, ‚though they searched, they etc.‘ or ‚they searched, but they etc.‘. Standing

---

*) This is not very carefully observed even in good mscr. and prints, where ཡང་ will occur sometimes after ག་ etc., and ཀྱང་ after the other consonants and even after vowels.

for itself (not leaning on the preceding word) it means ‚again, once more‘ (when it is to be regarded as adverb), དེར་ཡང་འཁམས་ནས་ , there (I) fainting once more etc.‘. In the beginning of a sentence it is ‚and, again, moreover‘, and may occasionally be rendered by ‚however, but‘. ཡང་ན་, ‚or‘; repeated, ཡང་ན་ ··· ཡང་ན་ ··· ‚either—or—‘. — ‚Or‘ is expressed also by the interrogative affix of the finite verb (34. 1.), འམ་ etc., གསེར་དངུལ་འམ། ཟངས་ ཀྱི་བུམ་པོ་ ‚a bottle of gold, silver, or copper‘. — འོན་ཀྱང་ ‚nevertheless, but‘, vulg: ཡིན་ཀྱང་ occurs much less frequently in Tibetan than in the European languages.

The only Subordinate Conjunctions are: 1. གལ་ཏེ་ ‚if‘, introducing conditional sentences ending in ན་ (40. 1. A. 4). But, as the conditional force really rests on the closing ན་, the initial གལ་ཏེ་ may be put or omitted at pleasure; 2. ཅི་སྟེ་ ‚but if‘; གལ་ཏེ་ནུས་ན་ ··· ‚if I can ...‘, ཅི་སྟེ་མི་ནུས་ན་ ‚but if not ...‘; this last is found only in books.

Chapter X.

The Interjection.

45. The most common Interjection is ཀྱེ་, or, repeated, ཀྱེ་ཀྱེ་ ‚oh!, alas!‘ used also before the Vocative. The language of common life uses instead: ཝ་ *wa*, or ཝའི་ *wä*.

Chapter XI.

Derivation.

46. Derivation of Substantives. As most of what belongs under this head has already been mentioned in 11. and 12. only the formation of abstract nouns remains to be spoken of. 1. The unaltered adjective may be used as an abstract noun, especially with the article བ་, as: གྲང་བ་རོ་བར་ འགྱུར་ ,the cold is changed into warmth'. — To this may be added the pronoun ཉིད་ (གྲང་བ་ཉིད་ ,ipsum frigidum'); but this is used scarcely anywhere else than in metaphysical treatises, from whence a few expressions, such as སྟོང་པ་ཉིད་ ,the vacuum, the absolute rest in deliverance from existence' have become more generally known. — 2. In the case of two correlative ideas existing, frequently the compound of both is used, esp. in common talk, ཆེ་ཆུང་ ,size' (lit. ,large and small'), སྦོམ་ཕྲ་ ,thickness' (,thick and thin'), e.g. ཆེ་ཆུང་ནི་ཡུངས་འབྲུ་ཙམ་ ,the size as much as a mustard-seed'. — 3. ཁྱད་ ,difference' (or, sometimes, ཚད་, ཆོད་ ,measure') is added, མཐོ་ཁྱད་ ,height', ཕྱུག་ཁྱད་ ,wealth, riches'. — 4. Mental qualities are in most cases paraphrased by སེམས་, or བློ་ with a genitive, བཟོད་པའི་སེམས་ ,mind of suffering, enduring, i.e. patience', མཁས་པའི་བློ་ ,wise mind, wisdom, skill'; དགའ་བའི་སེམས་ ,mind of rejoicing, joy' (vulg: སེམས་དགའ་མོ་), དད་པའི་སེམས་ ,mind of belief (also ,a believing mind'), faith'. — 5. Diminutives are formed by adding the termination འུ་, often with an alteration of the preceding vowel: རྟ་ ,horse', རྟེའུ་ ,little horse, foal'; མི་ ,man', མིའུ་ ,little man, dwarf'; རྡོ་ ,stone', རྡེའུ་ ,small stone, calculus'. If a word ends with a consonant, only *u* is added, and a new syllable formed: ལུག་ ,sheep', ལུ་གུ་ ,lamb'.

47. Derivation of Adjectives.

1. Possessive adjectives are regularly expressed by adding the syllable ཅན་, or the phrase དང་ལྡན་པ་, abridged ལྡན་ to any substantive, མགོ་ ཅན་ ,having a head'; མི་མགོ་ཅན་ ,having the head of a man'; སྐྲ་ཅན་ ,having hair, (long-) haired'; རིག་པ་ཅན་, རིག་པ་ དང་ལྡན་པ་ ,possessing knowledge, learned, wise'; དང་ལྡན་ པ་ is never heard in common talk in WT. — 2. Adjectives of appurtenance are generally expressed by the genitive of the substantive, གསེར་གྱི་ ,of gold, golden'; འདི་མིག་ ,the eye of flesh, the carnal, bodily eye', oppos.: ཤེས་རབ་ཀྱི་མིག་ ,the eye of knowledge, spiritual eye'. — 3. Negative, or privative adjectives are formed in several ways: *a*) by the simple negative མི་, མི་འོས་པ་ ,unworthy'; མི་རུང་བ་ ,unfit'; མི་ཐོས་པ་ ,unheard of'. *b*) by adding མེད་ ,without'

མགོ་མེད་ ‚headless'; སྐྱོན་མེད་ ‚faultless'. *c*) by adding the verb བྲལ་(བ་) ‚separated from', ལུས་དང་བྲལ་བ་, ལུས་བྲལ་ ‚separated from the body, bodiless'. — 4. The English adjectives in *-able*, *-ible* are expressed by རུང་བ་ ‚to be fit', added to the Supine, or to the simple Root, འཐུང་དུ་རུང་བ་, འཐུང་རུང་ ‚fit for drinking, drinkable', vulgo: འཐུང་ཉན་ (from ཉན་པ་ ‚to be able'), འཐུང་ཆོག་ (ཆོག་ ‚permitted, lawful').

Part III.

Syntax.

48. Arrangement of words. 1. The invariable rule is this: in a simple sentence all other words must precede the verb; in a compound one all the subordinate verbs in the form of gerunds or supines, and all the coordinate verbs in the form of the root, each closing its own respective clause, must precede the governing verb (examples s. below). — 2. The order in which the different cases of substantives belonging to a verb are to be arranged, is rather optional, so that e.g. the agent may either precede or follow its object. Local and temporal adverbs or adverbial phrases are, if possible, put at the head of the sentence. — 3. The order of words belonging to a substantive is this: 1 The Genitive, 2. the governing Substantive, 3. the Adjective (unless this is itself put, in the genitive, before; 16), 4. the Pronoun, 5. the Numeral, 6. the indefinite Article: thus, ངའི་བུ་མོ་ཆུང་ ང་འདི་ ‚this my little daughter'; གོས་དམར་པོ་ཞིག་ ‚a red gown'; གོས་དམར་པོ་ or དམར་པོ་དེ་གོས་ ‚the red gown'; རྒྱལ་ཁམས་ཆེན་པོ་འདི་གསུམ་ ‚these three great kingdoms'. Adverbs precede the word they belong to: ཤིན་ཏུ་ཆེན་པོ་ ‚very great'; ཤིན་ཏུ་མགྱོགས་པར་ཤོག་ ‚come very quickly'. —

4. In correlative sentences (cf. 29) the Relative precedes the Demonstrative: གང་ཡོད་པ་དེ་སྟོང་ཞིག་ ‚what there is, give!‘ i. e. ‚give whatever you have‘, and in comparative sentences the thing with which another is compared, ordinarily precedes this (cf. 17).

49. Use of the cases. As the necessary observations about the instrumental have been made in 30, about the other cases and postpositions partly in 15, partly in 43, it is only the Accusative, that requires a few words more, as it is very often used absolutely (as in Greek). *a*) Acc. temporalis: མཚན་མོ་ ‚at night‘; གསོན་པོ་དེའི་ཚེ་ ‚during (his etc.) lifetime‘; དེའི་ཚེ་, དེ་དུས་ ‚at that time‘; ཉི་མ་གཅིག་བསླབས་ནས་ ‚having studied for one day, after one day's study‘. — *b*) Acc. modalis: དབྱིབས་ཟླུམ་པོ་ ‚regarding the size, round‘; གཏིང་ཟབ་ཁྲུ་ཁྱ་བརྒྱད་པ་ ‚regarding the depth, eight cubits‘ (cf. 12); ཁ་དོག་དུ་བ་ལྟ་བུར་ཡོད་པ་ ‚regarding colour, being like smoke‘ (cf. 50, 1, *a*); རིགས་མཐུན་པ་ ‚with regard to (his) birth, equal‘ i. e. ‚of equal birth‘. Here ནི་ (42. 1) is very often employed: དབྱིབས་ནི་ཟླུམ་པ་ etc. Nearly in all cases, however, postpositions may be added, and in talking they are preferred to the simple Accusative: མཚན་མོ་ལ་, མཚན་ལ་, དེའི་ཚེ་ན་, དབྱིབས་ལ་ etc.

50. Simple Sentences. — 1. A f f i r m a t i v e sentences.
— *a*) the attribute being a noun, the verb: *to be, become, remain* etc.: མི་འདི་ནི་མཁས་པ་ཡིན ,this man is wise'; འདི་ ནི་མི་མཁས་པ་ཞིག་ཡིན ,this is a wise man'. When the verb is འགྱུར་བ་ (to become), གནས་པ་ (to remain) etc. the attribute must be put in the Terminative: སྐྲ་དཀར་པོར་གྱུར་ཏོ ,(his) hair became white'; རྒྱལ་པོ་ཡི་དམ་ལ་བརྟན་པར་གནས་ སོ, vulg: བརྟན་པོ་གནས་པ་ཡིན ,the king remained steadfast on his vow'; in some special cases this may take place, even if the verb is simply ,to be': ལུས་གཟུགས་ ཐམས་ཅད་མི་འདྲ་སྟེ། རྐང་པ་འབའ་ཞིག་ཁྲ་བོར་འདུག་གོ ,while his whole shape was like a man's, his foot only was piebald'. *b*) the attribute being any other verb: རྒྱ་ནག་ཡུལ་ གྱི་རྒྱལ་པོ་སྔ་མ་ཞིག་གིས་ཡུལ་དེའི་བྱང་ཕྱོགས་སུ་ལྕགས་རི་ཤིན་ཏུ་ ཆེན་པོ་ཞིག་བརྩིགས་སོ ,an ancient king of China built a very large wall in the north of that country'.

2. I n t e r r o g a t i v e s e n t e n c e s. — *a*) simple: ཁྱོད་ཀྱི་ བུ་ཁང་པ་ལ་འདུག་གམ ,is your son in the house?'; དེ་ རུ་སུ་ ཡོད་ ,who is there?'; ཅི་ལ་ཡོང་ ,what do you come for?', ,what do you want?'. — རིན་ཚམ W (རིན་ག་ཚོད C) ,how much (is) the price?'.

Besides the affix *am* the later literature and the conversational language of CT has the accentuated interrogative particle ཨེ *ĕ*, immediately before the verb: ཐབས་ཨེ་ཡོད་ *ťab ĕ yö*᾿ ‚is there any means ....?‘; ལས་འདི་བྱེད་ཨེ་ནུས་ *lǎ di jĕ ĕ nǔ* ‚can you do this work?‘.

The form of a question is also used to express uncertain suppositions (likely to become realized), as: བརྗེད་པ་སྲིད་དམ་ ‚is forgetting possible?‘ for ‚he may possibly have forgotten it‘; ཤི་བ་ཡིན་ནམ་ ‚won't he die?‘; འདི་བདུད་མ་ཡིན་ནམ་ ‚this (apparition) is not the devil, I hope?‘.

b) double: ནང་ན་ཡོད་དམ་མེད་ ‚is (he) within or not?‘; བདག་ལ་སྤྲིན་དུ་རུང་ངམ་མི་རུང་ ‚is it agreeable (to you i. e. do you consent) to give me (your son) or not?‘; ང་འོངས་པ་མི་ དགའ་འམ་ཅི་ཉེས་ ‚are you sorry at my arrival, or what (else) is the matter (with you — because you weep)?‘.

3. Imperative and Optative or Precative sentences do not require any additional remarks besides what is said in 38.

51. Compound Sentences. After having examined in 41 the different gerunds as the constituent parts of compound sentences, a few examples will suffice for illustration.

1. Compound sentences, for the most part coordinative: རྒྱལ་པོས་ཁྲིམས་བཅའ་སྟེ[1]། བཟང་[2]ལ་བྱ་དགའ་སྟེར། ངན་པ་ལ་

---

1) འཆའ་བ་, perf. བཅའ་ ‚to make‘ esp. ‚institute,

ཆད་པ་གཅོད[3] ། བྱེ་སྲང་གཏན་ལ་ཕབ[4] ། མི་ལ་ཡི་གེ་བསླབས་སོ[5] །།

,The king having given a law, the good were given rewards,
the bad punished, measures and weights arranged, and
people taught letters (i. e. reading and writing)'.

2. subordinate sentences: དེར[1] བུད་མེད་གཉིས་ཤིག[2] བུ

གཅིག་ལ་རྩོད་དེ། རྒྱལ་པོ་ཌྲོ[3] མཁས་པས་བཏག་ནས[4] འདི་སྐད་

ཅེས[5] བསྒོ་འོ། །ཁྱེད་གཉིས་ཀྱིས་བུའི་ལག་པ་རེ་རེ་ནས་བཟུང་སྟེ།

དོངས་ལ[6] གང་གིས་ཐོབ་པ[7] བུ་ཁྱེར་ཞིག[8] ཅེས་བསྒོ་བ་དང[9] ། བུའི

མ་མ་ཡིན་པ་དེས་ནི[10] བུ་ལ་སྙིང་རྗེ་མེད་པས[11] སྲད་ཀྱིས[12] མི་དོགས་

ཏེ། མཐུ་རྗེ་ཡོད་པར[13] དྲངས་སོ། །བུའི་མ་གང་ཡིན་པ་དེ་ནི་བུ་ལ

བྱམས་པས་སྲད་ཀྱིས་དོགས་ཏེ། ཕོབས་ཀྱིས་ཐུབ་ཀྱང[14] དྲག་ཏུ[15]

---

arrange'; gerund.　2) i. o. བཛང་པོ་ལ་.　3) ,to cut', but ཆད་

པ་ (or པས་) གཅོད་པ་ ,to inflict a punishment'.　4) གཏན་

ལ་འབེབས་པ་ ,to set in order, arrange'; perf. ཕབ་.　5) སློབ་

པ་, perf. བསླབས་ ,to learn'.

1) 42. 3.　2) indefin. art. after numerals s. 13.　3) Accus. modal., 49.　4) དོག་པ་, perf. བཏག་.　5) 27. 2.　6) འདེན་
པ་, perf. དྲངས་, imp. དྲོངས་; cf. 41. 5.　7) 29.　8) འཁྱེར་
བ་, perf. and imp. ཁྱེར་.　9) 43. 1.　10) 42. 1.　11) 41. 8.
12) the object of the fear usually in the instrumental.　13) termin. of inf used as adverb, 41. B. 2. *b*.　14) 44.　15) 42. 2.

མ་[16] དངས་སོ། །རྒྱལ་པོས་དྲག་ཏུ་དངས་པ་དེ་ལ། འདི་ནི་ཁྱོད་ཀྱི་ བུ་མ་ཡིན་ཏེ། བུད་མེད་ཅིག་གཞན་[17] གྱི་བུ་ཡིན་པས་ན་[18]། དྲང་ པོར་[19] སྨྲོས་ཤིག་[20] ཅེས་སྨྲས་པ་དང་། དལ་གྱིས་དངས་པའི་བུ་ ཡིན་པར་གྱུར་ཏེ་[21] བུ་ཁྱེར་རོ༔ ,There being certain two women quarrelling about one boy, the king (being) wise of understanding having examined (the case) thus ordered: You two, having seized from each (side) a hand of the boy, pull, and who gets him, (she) may carry him off. — When he had so spoken, she who was not the boy's mother, because she had no compassion for the boy, not fearing (she might) hurt (him), pulled with what force she had. She who (in truth) was the boy's mother, because she had compassion with the boy, fearing (she might) hurt (him), though she was able by force, did not pull hard. The king said to her who had pulled hard: Because this, not being your son, is the other woman's son, say (it) outright'. When he had so spoken, as he had turned out to be the son of the gentle puller, (she) carried off the boy'.

---

16) 42. 1.   17) གཞན་ ,other', almost always with the in-defin. article; 13. fin.   18) ན་ is sometimes pleonastically added to པས་ (བས་), to strengthen its meaning.   19) 43. 2.
20) སྨྲ་བ་, perf. སྨྲས་, imp. སྨྲོས་.   21) འགྱུར་བ་, perf. གྱུར་ properly ,as he has come to be'.

Appendix.

A collection of phrases from daily life, in the modern dialects, romanized.

WT	*k̓yod gá-nạ yoṅ,*	Where do you come from?
CT	*k̓yö' ǵá-nạ yoṅ.*	
W	*k̓yod su yin,* C *k̓yö' s. y.*	Who are you?
W	*k̓yod (C k̓yö') sụ̄[1]) yin.*)*	Whose (man, servant) are you?
W	*k̓yod ráṅi miṅ ċi zer,*	What is your name?
C	*k̓yö'-kyi miṅ-la ǵan zér-gi yö'-d̓am.*	(rule 34. 2. *c* is not always observed)
W	*k̓yód-di k̓áṅ-pa ǵá-na yod,*	Where is your house?
C	*k̓yö'-kyi k̓aṅ-pa ǵá-na yö'(-pa).*	
W	*k̓yod ċi-la yoṅ,*	Why do you come?
C	*k̓yö' ǵaṅ-la yoṅ.*	(What do you want?)
W	*ċi-la 'i-ru dug.*	Why are you here?
W	*ṅa šruṅ-te dad.*	I sit here to watch.
W	*dī yúl-li miṅ ċi zer,*	What is the name of this village?
C	*yul dī miṅ-la ǵan zér-ra**) yim-pa.*	

---

*) The numbers refer to the notes at the end of the collection, exhibiting the spelling of some of the words that are most disfigured in pronunciation.

**) vulgar supine 41, Note 1.

W *ḱyod-la ḍel-wa²) żig yód-da,*
C *ḱyö' la ḍon żig yö'-ḍam.*
  Have you any errand (business)?

W *čaṅ med; čón-la yoṅ(s),*
C *čaṅ mě'; ḍon-mě'-la yoṅ.*
  Not any; I have come to no purpose.

W *da ṫug pa ṫuṅ-če-la kaṅ-pa-la-soṅ.*
  Then go home to eat (drink) your soup.

W *yod: ṅá-la man³) żig sal⁴),*
C *yö': ṅá-la man żig naṅ-⁵) rog.*
  Yes: please give me some medicine.

W *ṅá-la zug⁶) yod, Ts sug gyág⁷)-gī,*
Ü *ṅá-la ná-ṫsa toṅ⁸)-gi dug.*
  I am ill (I have got, am befallen with, an illness)

W *zúr-mo rag, C - - dug.*
  I feel pain.

W *gá-na, C ǵá-na.*
  Where?

W *ḍód-pa⁹)-la, C ḍö'-pa-la.*
  In the stomach.

W *gó-la zug rag, C - - - yö'.*
  I have headache.

W *ṅa-ża yaṅ-pa-la ča-če-la ṫsan-te rag.*
  We should have taken a walk, but it is too hot.

WC *di len.*
  Take this!

W *di ḱyer, C di ḱur soṅ.*
  Take this with (you)!

W *di ḱyoṅ, C di ḱur żog.*
  Bring this!

W *di gá-zug čo-če, C di ǵán-ḍa¹⁰) jě' toṅ (or jě' gyu) yin (yim-pa).*
  How shall I do this?

W *dí-zug čo mi gos (goi, gọ),*
C *dí-ḍā jě' mi gọ.*
  You must not do it in this way.

W *ńá-la da-ruṅ ó-ma žig gos,*

C *ńá-la ďa-ruṅ wó-ma šig gọ̈.*

I want some more milk.

W *i lág-mo čo,* C *di lég-mo ĵạ̈.*

Clean this!

W *bé-ma daṅ ṭu*[11])*-če,*
C *ĵé-mạ̈ ṭụ.*

Wash it with sand!

W *ńa-la ču čuṅ zad* (C *sä̌*) *čig naṅ*[12]) *žig* (C *šig*).

Give me some water, please!

W *lág-pa lág-mo yód-da,*
C *lág-pa lég-mo (lạ̈-mo, or tsaṅ-wa) é yö̌.*

Are (your) hands clean?

W *o-ma ťsag-rạ̈-la ťsag toṅ,*

C *wo-ma - - - ťsag šog.*

Filter the milk through the filtering cloth!

W *ťab čuṅ-se ďé̌ čog-la bor-toṅ,* C *- - - ďé̌ čog (čȫ)-la žag*[13])*-čig.*

Put the little stove there!

W *p̓àn-dil sá-la p̓ob*[14]) *(p̓ab-toṅ),*

C *saṅ*[15]) *sá-la p̓áb-šig.*

Put the pot (*degči*) down on the ground!

W *zaṅ(-bu) me daṅ ñe-mo bor,*

C *saṅ me ďaṅ ñe-mo žag.*

Put the pot near the fire!

W *p̓og ton.*

Take it off!

W *ñí-ma gás*[16])*-sa (gạ̈-a) tsám-žig-ga me p̓u*[17]),
C *- - gạ̈ tsam-šig-la - -.*

As soon as the sun sets, light a fire!

W *kar-yol k̓yoṅ-na son.*

Go to fetch the china!

- - len-na šog.

Come to take away - -.

W *ču ḍán-mo*[18]) *daṅ ṭú-na*
　kar-yól[19]) *mi dag* (or
　kar-yol lag-mo mi ča-
　yin); *t́sán-te žig lán-*
　te gyal-la ṭu gos (gǭ),

C *ču ḍáṅ mǭ ṭǖ na kar-yól*
　mi dag; t́sǎm-mo šig
　gī lég (lā̆)-pa- ṭǖ šog.

If you wash with cold water,
the china does not become
clean; wash it well with
some hot (water)!

W *lás (lā̆)-ka t́saṅ-ma t́sar-*
　nạ mán-na ma ča,

C - - - *mạm-pa ḍo*[20]) *mi*
　čog.

Unless all the work is done,
don't go! (or) you must
not go.

W *sol-čóg*[21]) *t́al-ḍig*[22]) *čo-a,*

C - - - - *žě' gyu yin-na(m).*

Shall I make the table ready?

W *o-ná; čog-tán tiṅ*[23]) *toṅ,*

C *yā̆-ya; čog-tán tíṅ-čig.*

Yes; lay (spread) the
cloth!

W *tib-ril li naṅ-na ču mán-*
　po yód-da ñúṅ-ñu yód,

C - - *gyi-naṅ-na ču mán-*
　po yö'-ḍam ñúṅ-ñu yö'.

Is there much water in the
teapot, or little?

W *ñúṅ ñu žig yod (a-t́sig*
　man-na med),

C *ñúṅ ñu šig yö'.*

(But) a little.

W *tib-ril ču kaṅ*[24])-*te ḱyoṅ,*

C - - *čǖ ḱạṅ-nā̆ ḱur šog.*

Fill the teapot with water,
and bring it!

W *tib-ril dzag dug.*

The kettle leaks.

W *kár-yā̆*[25]) *daṅ j̇ar*[26]) *gos*
　(gǭ),

C *kár-yā̆ (or ša-kar-gyī)*
　j̇ar gǭ.

It must be soldered (fastened
with pewter).

W *gar-wạ*[27]) *tsar*[28]) *ḱyer,*

C *ḱur soṅ.*

Take it to the blacksmith's.

W *šel-kor gas (gā̌) soṅ,*
C *šel-p̓or gā̌ soṅ.*

The tumbler (glass-cup) has got a crack.

W *ṅā̌mazer-na šiṅmak̓yoṅ,*
C *- - ser-na - - kyal²⁹).*

Unless I tell you, do not bring wood!

W *sab mol-na k̓yoṅ yin,*
C *sa-hib suṅ³⁰)-na kyal gyu yin.*

When master commands, I shall bring.

W *sab gȧ-zug mol,* C *sa-hib g̓aṅ suṅ wa yin.*

What did you say, sir (did the gentleman say)?

W *ma p̓aṅ³¹); budmačug³²),*
C *ma b̓or-wa ǰĕ'; b̓ü' ma čug.*

Don't cast it away! Do not let it slip!

WC *rig-pa ḍim³³),* W *k̓a-dar čo.*

Take care! Cautiously!

W *nȧn³⁴)-če man,*
C *nȧṅ gyu min.*

You must not press!

W *ḍȧs³⁵)-si (ḍȧ̌-i) lȧg-ma ṭi³⁶)-te bor,*
C *ḍȧ̌-kyi lhȧg-ma t̓sag ǰȧ̌.*

Put by the remainder of the rice!

W *lag-ma mi dug, čaṅ ma lus (lū̌).*

There is no remainder, nothing is left.

W *o-ma lud ma čug,*
C *wo-ma lü' ma čug.*

Do not let the milk run over!

W *čin-pa³⁷) ma túb³⁸)-te són-te k̓yoṅ,*
C *- - - - - t̓sȧṅ-ma (or g̓ȧṅ-mo) k̓ur-šog.*

Not cutting the liver, bring it as a whole!

W *a-lu šu-te tub toṅ,*
C *kyi-u (or ḍo-ma³⁹) šu-te tub-čig.*

Peel the potatoes, and cut them in pieces!

maṅ-po (or yun riṅ-mo) ma gor.

Don't tarry much!

W *gyog-pa* (C *gyog-po, gyō-po*) *šog.*	Come soon!
W *ma jed*[40]), C *ma jĕ'.*	1. Do not forget! 2. (I) did not forget.
W *yid-la zum*[41]) *ťub-ba,* C *sem-la ñē ťub-ba.*	Can you remember it (bear it in mind)?
W *yid-la zum gos* (*gọ*), C *ñē-pa jĕ' gọ.*	You must bear it in mind, (make it certain).
nan-du son; nan-du šog.	Go in! Come in!
W *nan-du kyod*[42]), C *nan-du peb.*	Go (or come) in, sir!
W *dod*[43]), C *dä'.*	Sit down!
žug[44]).	Please sit down, sir!

---

1) སུའི་ 2) བྲེལ་བ 3) སྐུན 4) སུ་ལ 5) གནང 6) གཟུག

7) རྐུག 8) གཏོང 9) གྱོད 10) ག་འདྲས 11) འཁྱུ 12) གནང

13) བཞག 14) འབེབས་པ iprv. 15) ཟངས 16) ནུས

17) འབུད་པ iprv. 18) གང་མོ 19) དགར་ཡོལ 20) འགྲོ

21) གསོལ་ཁྲུག 22) འཕུལ་འགྲུག 23) བཏི prf. of འདི་ང་བ

24) བགང prf. of འགོངས་པ 25) དགར་གཡའ 26) སྐུར

prf. of སྐུར་བ 27) མགར་བའི 28) ཅུར 29) བསྐུལ prf. of

སྐུལ་བ 30) གསུང 31) འཕང iprv. of འཕེན་པ 32) བཅུག

prf. of འཇུག་པ 33) འགྲེམ 34) གནན 35) འབྲས 36) དཀྱི

37) མཆིན་པ 38) བཅུབ prf. of འཕུབ་པ 39) གོམ 40) རྗེད

41) རྗུམ i.o. བཟུང from འཛིན་པ 42) སྐྱོད 43) སྡོད 44) བཞུགས

Reading Exercise.

The Story of *Yug-pa-ċan* the Brahman [1].

༄༅། །ཁྱུལ་ཞིག[2] ན[3] བྲམ་ཟེ་དབྱུག་པ་ཅན་ཞེས་བྱ་བ[4] ཞིག
འདུག[5]སྟེ[6]། རབ་ཏུ་དབུལ་འཕོངས་པ་བཟའ་བ་དང་། བགོ་བ་མེད་
པ་[7]ཞིག་གོ[8]། དེས་ཁྱིམ་བདག་ཅིག་ལས[9]བ་གླང་ཞིག་བཅུས་ཏེ།
ཉིན་པར་སྐྱུང་ནས་བ་གླང་དེ་ཁྱེར་དེ་ཁྱིམ་བདག་དེའི་ཁྱིམ་དུ་ཕོང་བ
དང་། དེན[10]ཁྱིམ་བདག་ནི་ཟན་ཟ་སྟེ། དབྱུག་པ་ཅན་གྱིས་བ་གླང་དེ
ཁྱིམ་གྱི་ནང་དུ་བཏང[11]བ་དང་། བ་གླང་སྒོ་གཞན་དུ་ཕོང་ནས་ཕྱིར་རོ།།
ཁྱིམ་བདག་དེ་ཟན་དེ་ཟོས་ནས་ལངས[12]པ་དང་། དེན་བ་གླང་མ
མཐོང་ནས་དེས་དབྱུག་པ་ཅན་ལ་གླང་ག་རེ་ཞེས་བྱས་པ[13]དང་། དེས

---

1) From the *Dzaṅ-lun* (མཛངས་བླུན). — 2) 13. —
3) 15, 5. — 4) བྱེད་པ, perf. བྱས, fut. བྱ, iv. བྱོས,to make,
do' in some cases: ,to say, call', ཞེས་བྱ་བ ,so to be called,
so called'. — དབྱུག་པ་ཅན is a translation of the Sanscrit
name དཎྜིན. — 5) 40. 1. *c*. — 6) 41. A. 1. — 7) 40.1. *b*
and 47. 3. *b*. — 8) 34. 1. and 40. 1. *g*. — 9) 15. 5. —
10) 42. 3. — 11) perf. of གཏོང་བ ,to give; to send, let go'.
— 12) perf. of ལང་བ ,to rise'. — 13) s. 4). —

སྐྱེས་པ། ཁྱོད་ཀྱི་ཁྲིམས་དུ་བདང་ངོ་། །ཁྱོད་ཀྱིས་འདི་སྐྱང་བོར་ཀྱིས[14] སྐྱར་བྱིན་ཅིག[15] ཅེས་སྐྱས་པ་དང་། དེས་སྐྱས་པ། ངས་མ་བོར་རོ།། དེ་ནས་དེ་གཉིས་འགྲོགས་ཏེ། རྒྱལ་པོ་འི་ཐད་དུ་འདོང་བ་དང་། ཅུ་བུ་ཙག་གི་རིགས་པ་དང་མི་རིགས་པ་རྟོག་པར་འགྱུར་རོ[16] ཞེས་སྐྱས་ནས་དེ་གཉིས་རོང་བ་དང་། མི་གཞན་ཞིག་གི་རྟ་ཤོར་མ་ཞིག་ཐོས་ནས། དེས་དྲུག་པ་ཅན་ལ་སྐྱས་པ། རྟོང་མ་མ་བདང[17] ཞེས་སྐྱས་པ་དང་། དེས་རོ་ཞིག་བླངས[18] ཏེ་འཕངས[19] པ་དང་དའི་ཀཾ་པ་ལ་ཕོག་ནས་ཀཾང་པ་བཅག[20] གོ །དེས་སྐྱས་པ། ཁྱོད་ཀྱིས་འདི་དུ་བསད་ཀྱིས[21] འདི་དུ་བྱིན་ཅིག །ཅིའི་ཕྱིར་དུ་སྨྲིན། དེས་སྐྱས་པ་ཅར་འོག །རྒྱལ་པོ་འི་དྲུང་དུ[22] འདོང་དང་། ཅུ་བུ་ཙག་གི་ལ་ཆེ་གཅོད་དུ་འོང་ངོ་ཞེས་སྐྱས་ནས། དེ་དག་དེར་སོང་བ་དང་། དབྱུག་པ་ཅན་དེས་འབྲོས་པར་བརྩམས[23] ཏེ། དེས[24] རྟེག་པ་ཞིག་གི

14) 41. A. 7. — 15) imp. of སྤྱིན་པ་ ,to give', སྐྱར་··· ,to return'. — 16) 37. 2. — 17) གཏོང་བ་ s. 11); ,don't let pass'; 38. 2. — 18) perf. of ལེན་པ་ ,take, seize'.— 19) perf. of འཕེན་པ་ ,to throw, fling'. — 20) perf. of གཅོག་པ་ , to break'. — 21) s. 14). — 22) 43. 2. — 23) perf. of རྩོམ་པ་ ,to prepare, purpose'. -- 24) rule 30. is not always strictly observed. —

སྟེང་ནས་²⁵ མཚོངས་པ་དང་། དེའི་དྲུང་ན་ཐག་པ་ཞིག་ཐགས་འཐག་
ཅིང་འདུག་པ་དེའི་སྟེང་དུ་ལྷུང་²⁶ ནས་ཐག་པ་དེ་ཚོ་འཕོས་པ་དང་། ཐ
ག་པའི་རྒྱང་མས་དབུག་པ་ཅན་དེ་བཟུང་²⁷ ནས། ཁྱོད་ཀྱིས་འདིའི་ཕོ
བསད་ཀྱིས་འདི་ཁྲིད་ཞིག་ཅེས་སྨྲས་པ་དང་། ངས་ཁྱོད་ཀྱི་ཁྲི་ཙེ
ལྱར་²⁸ སྟིན་ཞེས་སྨྲས་ནས། ཚར་ཕོག་རྒྱལ་པོ་དེ་དྲུང་དུ་འདོང་ངོ་།།
དེས་འུ་བུ་ཆག་གི་ཁལ་ཙེ་གཅད་དོ་ཞེས་དོང་བ་ལས།²⁹ ལམ་གྱི
བར་ན་རྩ་པོ་གཏིང་ཟབ་པོ་³⁰ ཞིག་ཡོད་དེ། རྒྱ་དེའི་ནང་ནས་ཚུར་³¹
ཕྱང་གཱནན་³² ཞིག་སྟེའུ་ཁ་ན་འཁྱེར་ཏེ་འོང་ངོ་། །དེ་ལ་དྲུག་པ
ཅན་གྱིས་རྒྱའི་གཏིང་ཙེ་ཚམ་ཞེས་དྲིས་³³ པ་དང་། རྒྱའི་གཏིང་ཟབ
པོ་³⁴ ཞེས་སྨྲས་པས་³⁵ སྟེའུ་རྒྱར་ལྷུང་སྟེ། སྟེའུ་མ་རྙེད་པ་དང་།
དེས་དྲུག་པ་ཅན་བཟུང་ནས། ཁྱོད་ཀྱིས་འདིའི་སྟེའུ་རྒྱར་བསྒྱུར་རོ་³⁶ །།
དེས་སྨྲས་པ་ངས་མ་བསྒྱུར་རོ། །ཚར་ཕོག་རྒྱལ་པོ་དེ་དྲུང་དུ
འདོང་དང་། དེས་འུ་བུ་ཆག་གི་ཁལ་ཙེ་གཅད་དོ་ཞེས་སྨྲས་ནས་དོང

---

25) 43. 2. — 26) perf. of ལྷུང་བ་ ‚to fall‘. — 27) perf.
of འཛིན་པ་ ‚to seize‘. — 28) 43. 2. *b.* — 29) 41. 6. *b*; ཞེས་
= ཞེས་སྨྲས་ནས་. — 30) 49.— 31) ‚from the inner (i.e. other)
side to this‘, ‚across‘. — 32) carpenter (lit. ‚*lakriwālā*‘, cf.
12. 1.). — 33) perf. of འདྲི་བ་ ‚to ask‘. — 34) 40. 1. *g.* —
35) 41. A. 8. — 36) perf. of སྒྱུར་བ་ ‚to throw down‘. —

ཧོ། །དེ་དག་སོང་བ་ལས་ ³⁷ རྒྱལ་པོ་འི་དྲུང་དུ་ཕྱིན་པ་དང་། དེ་
དག་རྒྱལ་པོ་འི་ཀང་པ་ལ་མགོ་བོས་ཕྱག་འཚལ་ཏེ། ཕྱོགས་གཅིག་
ཏུ་འདུག་གོ ³⁸ །དེ་ནས་རྒྱལ་པོས་དེ་དག་ལ་ཁྱོད་ཅི་ལ་འོངས་ཞེས་
དྲིས་པ་དང་། དེ་དག་གིས་དབྱུག་པ་ཅན་དང་ཁྱིམ་བདག་ཚོང་པ་ ³⁹
དེ་དག་ཐམས་ཅད་སྨྲས་སོ། །རྒྱལ་པོས་དབྱུག་པ་ཅན་ལ་སྨྲས་པ།
ཁྱོད་ཀྱིས་བླང་བཅས་སམ། །བཅས་སོ། །འོ་ན་ཕྱིར་ཕྱིན་ནམ།།
བདག་གིས་མ་ཕྱིང་བར་ ⁴⁰ བྱིན་ཏེ། །ཁས་ ⁴¹ ཉེ་མ་བཏང་ངོ་། །རྒྱལ་
པོས་སྨྲས་པ། དབྱུག་པ་ཅན་ཉེས་ལྟང་ཕྱིར་ཕྱིན་ཏེ་མ་སྨྲས་པས་ན་ ⁴²
སྐྱེ་ཚོར་ཅིག །ཁྱིམ་བདག་ཀྱང་ལྟང་འོངས་པར་ ⁴³ མཐོང་ལ་ ⁴⁴ མ་
བདགས་ ⁴⁵ པས་ནི། སྨིག་ཕྱུང་ ⁴⁶ ཞིག་ཅེས་བཅོད་དོ། །ཁྱིམ་བདག་
གིས་སྨྲས་པ། དབྱུག་པ་ཅན་གྱིས་གཅིག་ཏུ་ ⁴⁷ དེ་བདག་གི་ ⁴⁸ ལྟང་

---

37) s. 29). — 38) ‚sat down'. — 39) if the verb is in
the infv., the subject is usually put in the accus., when we
use the genitive. — 40) ‚returning it so that the owner
saw it'; 41. B. 2. *b.* — 41) ‚I did not return it with the
mouth i. e. by saying anything'. — 42) ‚because (41. A. 8)
that Yugp. did not say it (viz: I give back)'. — 43) 41. B.
2. *a.* — 44) 41. A. 5. — 45) perf. of འདོགས་པ་ ‚to tie,
fasten'. — 46) impv. of འབྱིན་པ་ ‚to take out, pull out' etc.
— 47) ‚firstly', less frequent and somewhat different from
དང་པོར་ (22). — 48) ‚my' (24). —

ཕྱོགས། གཉིས་སུ་[49] བདག་གི་མིག་ཕྱུང་བ་བས་[50]། དགྲ་པ་
ཅན་རྒྱལ་བར་འགྱུར་ཡང་སྣྱེན་[51]། མི་གཅིག་གིས་སྨྲ་[52]། དགྲ་
པ་ཅན་གྱིས་བདག་གི་ཊ་གོང་མ་བཀུམ་[53] མོ་ཞེས་སྨྲས་པ་དང་། རྒྱལ་
པོས་དགྲ་པ་ཅན་ལ་ཁྱོད་ཀྱིས་ཊ་ཅི་ལྟར་བསད་ཅེས་དྲིས་ནས། །
བདག་ལག་དུ་ཞུགས་[54] ཏེ་མཆེས་པ་ལས། མི་འདིས་ཊ་མ་བདང་
ཞེས་མཆི་[55] བ་ལས། བདག་གིས་རོ་ཞིག་སྐྲས་ཏེ། འཕངས་པ་
ལ་[56] ཊ་བཀུམ་མོ། །རྒྱལ་པོས་སྨྲས་པ། ཊ་བདག་གིས་ཊ་མ་བདང་
ཞེས་སྨྲས་པས་སྤྱི་ཚོང་ཅིག །དགྲ་པ་ཅན་ནི་[57] རོ་འཕངས་པས་
ལག་པ་ཚོང་ཅིག །མི་དེས་སྨྲས་པ། གཅིག་ཏུ་བདག་གི་ཊ་བསད།
གཉིས་སུ་བདག་གི་ལྟེ་གཅད་པ་བས། །དགྲ་པ་ཅན་རྒྱལ་བར་
འགྱུར་ཀྱང་སྣྱེན། །ཐག་པའི་ཚུང་མས་སྨྲས་པ། དགྲ་པ་ཅན་

---

49) ‚secondly‘. — 50) 17. 1. — 51) ‚it is better that Y. should be the winner, than that besides having been robbed of my ox, I should lose my eyes into the bargain. — 52) ‚another said: O god! etc.‘ (སྨྲ used in addressing a king like Sanscr. དེབ). — 53) perf. of འགུམ་པ་ ‚to kill‘; འགུམ་པ་ ‚to die‘ has perf. གུམ་; an elegant word (24, Note). — 54) perf. of འཇུག་པ་ ‚to enter‘. — 55) མཆི་བ་ perf. མཆེས་ ‚to go, walk‘; eleg. ‚to say‘. — 56) 41. A. 5. b. — 57) Nomin. for Instrum., s. 30 fin. —

གྱིས་བདག་གི་ཁྲི་བཀུམ་མོ། །དྲུག་པ་ཅན་གྱིས་སྨྲས་པ། བདག་
ལ་དགུ་མངས་པས་[58]འཇིགས་ཏེ་ཉིགས་པ་ལས་བཀྲལ་ནས་བྲོས་པ་
ལས། ཕག་ན་མི་ཡོད་པ་[59]མ་མཐོང་སྟེ་གུམ་མོ། །རྒྱལ་པོས་སྨྲས་
པ། སོང་ལ་[60]འདི་ཉིད་[61]ཀྱི་ཁྲི་གྱིས་[62]ཤིག །དེས་སྨྲས་པ།
གཅིག་ཏུ་བདག་གི་ཁྲི་བསད། གཉིས་སུ་འདི་ཁྲི་བྱས་པ་བས་[63]།
དྲུག་པ་ཅན་རྒྱལ་པར་འགྱུར་ཀུང་སྲིད། །ཤིང་མཁན་གྱིས་སྨྲས་པ།
དྲུག་པ་ཅན་དེ་[64]བདག་ལ་ཅུའི་གཏིང་ཙེ་ཚམ་ཞེས་དྲིས་པས། ཁ་
ནས་སྟེའི་ཕོགས་པ་[65]ཅུར་ཟྱུང་ངོ༌། །རྒྱལ་པོས་སྨྲས་པ། ཇེ་ཇེ་
ཁྱེར་ཡང་ཕྱག་པ་ལ་བཀུར་བའི་རིགས་ཀྱི་[66]ཁ་ན་ཉིར་བས། ཤིང་
མཁན་གྱི་མ་དུན་པོ་གཉིས་ཚོག་ཅིག །དྲུག་པ་ཅན་ནི་ཅུའི་གཏིང་
ཟབ་བས་ཞེས་པས་[67]སྟེ་ཆོད་ཅིག །ཤིང་མཁན་གྱིས་སྨྲས་པ།

---

58) perf. of མང་བ་ ‚to be much, many; to become m‘.
— 59) partic., ‚that a man was concealed (behind it)‘. —
60) 41. A. 5. — 61) 27. 1. — 62) imper. of བགྱིད་པ་ eleg.
for བྱེད་པ་ ; ‚go and make the husband of this same (woman)‘.
— 63) ‚than that he should be (my) husband‘. — 64) s. 57).
— 65) partic., ‚the axe which I held from (i. e. with) my
mouth‘. — 66) 40. 3 ‚whatever things be carried, it being
right to carry them on the shoulder‘. — 67) for ཞེས་སྨྲས་
པས་ s. 29). —

གཅིག་ཏུ་བདག་གི་སྙིན་སྟོར། གཉིས་སུ་བདག་གི་སོ་བཅག་པ་བས།

དབུག་པ་ཚན་རྒྱལ་བར་འགྱུར་ཀྱང་སྙོའི། ˣ⁾   །དེ་དག་སོ་སོ་ནས་⁶⁸

ཞལ་ཆེ་བཅད་དེ། དབུག་པ་ཚན་ཉིས་པ་ཀུན་ལས་ཐར་རོ॥   ॥

---

68) ˙˙ སོ་སོ་ ,different, several', ˙˙ ནས་ — ,separately,
each for himself'. —

Buddha Sacrifices Himself to a Tigress

༄༅། །འདི་སྐད་བདག་གིས་ཐོས་པ་དུས་གཅིག་ན། བཅོམ་ལྡན་འདས་མཉན་དུ་ཡོད་པ་ན་རྒྱལ་བུ་རྒྱལ་
བྱེད་ཀྱི་ཚལ་མགོན་མེད་ཟས་སྦྱིན་གྱི་ཀུན་དགའ་ར་བ་ན་བཞུགས་སོ། །དེའི་ཚེ་བཅོམ་ལྡན་འདས་བསོད་སྙོམས་ཀྱི་
དུས་ལ་བབ་ནས། ཁམ་ཕྱབས་དང་ཆོས་གོས་གསོལ་ནས་ལྷུང་བཟེད་བསྣམས་ཏེ། ཀུན་དགའ་བོ་དང་བསོད་སྙོམས་ལ་
གཤེགས་སོ། །དེའི་ཚེ་ན་གྲོང་ཁྱེར་དེ་ན་རྐུན་མོ་ཞིག་ལ་བུ་ཁྲག་ཏུ་བཙ་བ་གཉིས་ཤིག་ཡོད་དེ། ཤིང་བདག་གིས་
ཟེན་ནས་ཉལ་ཆེ་བའི་མདུན་དུ་ཁྲིད་དེ། ཁྲིམས་དང་སྦྱང་ཚེ་བསད་པ་ལ་ཕྱག་ནས། རི་གས་དང་སྒྲོག་སྟེ་གསོད་
པའི་གནས་སུ་ཁྲིད་པ་ལས། བཅོམ་ལྡན་འདས་རྒྱང་མ་ནས་གཟིགས་པ་རྐུན་མོ་མ་སྨྲ་གསུམ་གྱིས་མཐོང་ནས།
སངས་རྒྱས་གཤེགས་པའི་ཕྱོགས་སུ་ཕྱག་འཚལ་ནས ༎ ལྷའི་ིན་ན་གཏོ་བོ་ཕྱགས་བཙེ་བར་དགོངས་ཏེ། བདག་གི་
བུ་འགུམ་པ་ལ་ཕྱག་པ་འདིའི་སྐྱབས་མཛད་དུ་གསོལ་ཞེས་སྨྲས་པ་དང་། བཅོམ་ལྡན་འདས་ཀྱི་གསན་ནས། དེ་བཞིན་
གཤེགས་པའི་ཕྱགས་རྗེ་ཆེན་ཡོས། དེ་དག་ལ་ཕྱགས་བཙེ་བར་དགོངས་ཏེ། དེ་དག་གི་སྲོག་བསྐྱབས་པའི་སླད་དུ་
བཅོམ་ལྡན་འདས་ཀྱིས་ཀུན་དགའ་བོ་ལ་བཀའ་སྩལ་ཏེ། རྒྱལ་པོ་ལ་གསོལ་བ་འདེབས་སུ་བཏང་བ་དང་། རྒྱལ་
པོས་ཀྱང་བཅོམ་ལྡན་འདས་ཀྱི་བཀའ་བཞིན་དུ་དེ་དག་བཏང་ངོ་། །དེ་དག་བཅོམ་ལྡན་འདས་ཀྱི་བཀའ་དྲིན་དྲན་ཞིན་
རབ་ཏུ་དགའ་བ་སྐྱེས་ནས། བཅོམ་ལྡན་འདས་གང་ན་བ་དེ་ར་སོང་སྟེ་ཕྱིན་པ་དང་། ཞབས་ལ་སྤྱི་བོས་ཕྱག་འཚལ་
ནས་ཐལ་མོ་སྦྱར་དེ་བཅོམ་ལྡན་འདས་ལ་འདི་སྐད་ཅེས་གསོལ་ཏོ། །བཅོམ་ལྡན་འདས་ཀྱི་བཀའ་དྲིན་ཆེན་ཡོས་
བདག་ཅག་གི་ཚེ་སྲོག་ཐུག་མ་ཆེ་ཞིག་ལུས་པར་གྱུར་ན། ལྷའི་གཏོ་བོ་ཕྱགས་བཙེ་བར་དགོངས་ཏེ། བདག་ཅག་
ལ་ཚེར་ར་བ་དུ་འབྱུང་བར་ཚ་གཤེན་ཞེས་གསོལ་བ་དང་། བཅོམ་ལྡན་འདས་ཀྱིས་ལེགས་པར་འོངས་སོ་ཞེས་བཀའ་
སྩལ་པ་ན། སྐྲ་དང་ཁ་སྤུར་ད་ཕྱེ་སྟེ། གོས་ཀྱང་དར་སྐྱིག་ཏུ་གྱུར་ཏོ། །དེ་དག་ཀྱིན་དུ་དད་པའི་སེམས་བརྟན་
པར་གྱུར་ནས། བཅོམ་ལྡན་འདས་ཀྱིས་ཚེ་རིགས་པའི་ཆོས་བསྟན་ནས་རྒྱལ་དང་རི་མ་ཟད་དེ། དག་བཅོམ་པར་
གྱུར་ཏོ། །དེའི་མ་ཉན་མོ་དེ་ཡང་ཆོས་ཐོས་པས་ལན་གཅིག་ཕྱིར་མི་ལྡོག་པར་གྱུར་ཏོ། །དེའི་ཚེ་ཀུན་དགའ་བོས་
དེ་ལྟ་བུའི་དངོས་པོ་མཆར་ཆེ་བ་དག་མཐོང་ནས། དེ་བཞིན་གཤེགས་པའི་ཡོན་ཏན་དེ་སྐྱར་ཅིག་ལན་འི་ཞེས་བསྔགས་
ཏེ ༎ ཡང་འདི་སྙམ་དུ་ཉན་མོ་མ་སྨྲ་ད་གསུམ་པོ་འདིས་སྔོན་ལེགས་པ་ཅི་ཞིག་བགྱིས་ན་ད་ལྟར་བཅོམ་ལྡན་འདས་དང་
ཕྲད་དེ། ཉེས་པ་ཆེན་པོ་ལས་ཀྱང་ཐར་ལ། རྒྱ་འདན་ལས་འདས་པའི་བདེ་བ་ཐོབ་ནས་ལུས་གཅིག་གིས་ཐབ་པ་དང་།

བདེ་བའི་དོན་ཐོབ་པ་ལེགས་སོ་སྙམ་དུ་བསམ་པ་དང་། བཅོམ་ལྡན་འདས་ཀྱིས་མཐིན་ནས་ཀུན་དགང་པོ་ལ་འདི་
སྐད་ཅེས་བཀའ་སྩལ་ཏོ། །མ་སྐྱུར་གསུམ་པོ་འདི་ནི་ནས་དང་ལྫར་འདི་ལྦལ་ཝེག་གི་དུས་སུ་བསོས་པར་མ་ཟད་ཀྱི།
སྟོན་འདས་པའི་དུས་ན་ཡང་འདི་བཀལ་ངེན་གྱིན་གསོས་སོ། །ཀུན་དགང་པོ་གསོལ་པ། བཅོམ་ལྫན་འདས་སྟོན
འདས་པའི་དུས་ན་ཡང་མ་སྐྱུར་གསུམ་པོ་འདི་དག་ཆེ་ཀྱར་གསོས་པ་བཅོམ་ལྫན་འདས་ཀྱིས་བསྫན་དུ་གསོལ། བཅོམ
ལྫན་འདས་ཀྱིས་ཀུན་དགའ་པོ་ལ་བཀའ་སྩལ་པ། སྟོན་འདས་པའི་དུས་པ་བསྐལ་པ་གྲངས་མེད་པའི་ཕ་རོལ་ན།
འཛམ་བུའི་གླིང་འདི་ནི་རྒྱལ་པོ་ཁིང་ཙ་ཞེན་པོ་ཞེས་བྱ་བ་ཞིག་ཡོད་དེ་རྒྱལ་པོ་དེ་རྒྱལ་ཕྲན་ལྒ་སྟོང་སྟེང་ལ་དབང་བྱེད
དོ། །རྒྱལ་པོ་དེ་ལ་སྲས་གསུམ་མངའ་སྟེ། ར་བ་ནི་སྐྱུ་ཆེན་པོ་ཞེས་བྱའོ། །འབིང་པོ་ནི་ལྫ་ཆེན་པོ་ཞེས་བྱའི། །
ཐ་ཆུང་ནི་སེམས་ཅན་ཆེན་པོ་ཞེས་བྱ་སྟེ། སྲས་ཐ་ཆུང་དེ་རྒྱུ་དུ་ནས་བྱམས་པ་དང་སྙིང་རྗེ་ར་ལྫན་ཏེ། ཐབས
ཅན་ལ་བུ་ཆིག་པ་དང་འདྲའོ། །དེའི་ཚེ་རྒྱལ་པོ་དེ་བློན་པོ་དང་བཅས། བཙུན་མོ་དང་སྲས་སུ་བཅས་ཏེ། གྲེ
ཪོལ་དུ་འགྲག་ཅིང་དོང་བ་ལས། ཆུ་ཟད་ཅིག་འལ་བས་བྱེའི་བར་དུ་སྲས་གསུམ་པོ་ཚལ་གྱི་ནང་དུ་སོང་བ་ལས།
སྟག་མོ་ཞིག་བུ་བྱུང་ནས་དག་དུ་མ་ཝིན་པ་བགྱེས་ཤིང་སྲོལ་པས་ཉེན་ཏེ། བྱེར་ཡང་བུ་ཟོས་ལ་ཐུག་པ་ཞིག་མཐོང
ནས། རྒྱལ་བུ་ཐ་ཆུང་གིས་པོ་པོ་གཉིས་ལ་སྲས་པ། སྟག་མོ་འདི་ནི་ཤིན་དུ་སྲུག་བསྒལ་གྱིས་གཟིར་ཏེ། ཉུ་
ཆུང་ལ་རེད་པས་ཁི་ལ་ཕྲག་པ་འདི་ལྟ་བུ། ཕུ་བྱུང་མ་ཐག་པ་ཡང་ཟོས་སུ་ཉིང་དོ་ཞེས་སྨྲས་པ་དང་། པོ་པོ་གཉིས
ཀྱིས་ཁྱིད་ཟེར་བ་བདེན་ནོ་ཞེས་ཟེར་རོ། །དུ་པོས་ཡང་པོ་པོ་ལ་སྨྲས་པ། སྟག་མོ་འདིས་ཟས་སུ་ཅི་ཟ་ཞེས་ཉེས་ན།
པོ་པོ་གཉིས་ཀྱིས་སྨྲས་པ། འདི་བསད་མ་ཐག་པའི་ཤ་ཁྲོན་པ་དང་། ཞིག་དོན་ཨོས་དེའི་ཡིན་ཚོམ་པར་འགྱུར་རོ
ཞེས་སྨྲས་སོ། །ཡང་སྨྲས་པ་གང་ཤུ་ཡང་རུང་སྟེ། དེ་ལྟུ་ཕུའི་དོས་པོས་འདིའི་སྲོག་སྐྱབས་ཏེ། མི་ཉ་ཆས
པར་བྱེད་ནུས་པ་ཡོད་དམ། པོ་པོ་གཉིས་ཀྱིས་སྨྲས་པ། དེ་ནི་ཤིན་དུ་ཡང་དཀའ་བས་མེད་དོ། །དེ་ནས་རྒྱལ་བུ
ཐ་ཆུང་དེས་ཡིད་ལ་འདི་སྙམ་དུ་བསམས་སོ། །བདག་ཡུན་རིང་པོ་ནས་འཁོར་བ་ན་འཁོར་ཞིང་། ལུས་སྲོག
གྲངས་མེད་པ་ཞིག་ཆུད་གསན་ཏེ། བར་འགའ་ནི་འདོད་ཆགས་ཀྱི་ཕྱིར། བར་འགའ་ནི་ཞེ་སྫང་གི་ཕྱིར། བར
འགའ་ནི་གཏི་མུག་གི་ཕྱིར། ལུས་གཏང་ཡང་ཚོས་ཀྱི་ཕྱིར་བསོད་ནམས་ཀྱི་ཉིང་དང་། ལན་འགའ་ཡང་མ་བྱད་བའི
ལུས་འདི་ཅི་རུང་སྙམ་བསམ་ནས། གསུམ་ག་དབུགིགས་ཏེ་སོང་བ་དང་། རིང་པོར་མ་ཕྱིན་པར་པོ་པོ་གཉིས་ལ
འདི་སྐྱུར་ཅེས་སྨྲ་སོ། །མཁེད་གཉིས་སྱར་གཤེགས་ཤིག་དང་། བདག་དོ་ཞིག་གཉེ་ཏེ། སྐྱུར་བཞིན་པར

མ་ཆེའི་ཉེས་སྐྱོ་ས་སོ། །ལམ་ནེ་ཉིད་དུ་ཕྱུགས་ཏེ་སྒྲག་པོའི་ཆང་གང་དུ་ཡོད་པར་སྐྱུར་དུ་སོང་ནས། སྒྲག་མོའི་
རྦུང་དུ་ཁྱབ་པ་དང་། སྒྲག་མོ་ལ་ཐམས་པས་ཟ་ཀ་ནུས་སོ། །དེའི་ཚེ་རྒྱལ་པྲུས་ཀྱིང་ཀྱི་ཚལ་བ་ཏིད་པོར་འྱུས་ལ་
ཏིག་ཕྱུང་ནས། སྒྲག་མོ་ལ་བསྒྲག་དུ་བ་ཕྱག་པ་དང་། ཁ་ཡང་ཕྱི་ནས་འྱུས་ཏེ་ཀ་མ་འྱུ་པར་ཟིས་སོ། །
པོ་བོ་གཉིས་ཀྱིས་བཞུས་ན། རེང་ཉིག་དུ་མ་ཞིངས་པས། ཕྱིན་རྟིས་བ་ནེས་དུ་ཚིག་དུ་དོང་བ་ལས་སྒྱུ་དུ་སྐྱུ་བའི་
ཚལ་བདུག་ད་གཏན་མི་ཟ་པར་སྒྲག་མོ་ལྡོག་པས་བསད་དེ་བསམས་ནས་དེ་ར་ཕྱེད་དེ་བཞྱུས་ན། དུའི་བ་རྒྱུན་སྒྲག་
གིས་ཟོས་ཏེ། པ་དང་ཁག་གིས་ཀྱུད་དུ་བསྒྱི་པ་ནས། རྱག་རྟི་ག་པར་འདྱག་པར་མཐོང་ངོ་། །ལུས་ས་ལ་བརྡབས་ཏེ་
བརྒྱལ་ལོ། །རེང་ཉིག་ལྡིན་པ་དང་། དཔྱགས་ཕྱིར་བྱུང་ནས། ཆེ་ཉིས་འདེབས་ཏེ་ས་ལ་འགྲོ་ཞིང་ཀ་ཁྱམས་
པར་བྱུར་ཏོ། །དེའི་ཚེ་ར་བ་ཆུན་མོ་ཡུམ་མཁལ་པའི་སྐྱེ་ལ་གར་ན། སྒྱུ་རྟོ་ག་སྐྱུམ་ཉིག་ཀྱུན་དུ་བྱུ་ནིང་ཆེ་བ་
ལས། ནང་གི་ཀྱུན་དུ་ཉེག་ཞིས་ཆྱེར་བ་སྒྲག་སྒྱེས་མ་ཕག་དུ་སད་ནས། སྒྲག་དྲངས་དེ་རྒྱལ་པོ་ལ་བསྡུ་ཏོ། །
བདག་གིས་ཀ་ཏུམ་དུ་ཕེས་ན། སྒྱག་རྟོ་ནི་བུ་པོའི་ལྷ་སྟེ། དཀག་རྟོ་ན་ནང་གི་ཀྱུན་དུ་ཁྱམས་ཕྱིར་བ་ན། བདག་གི་
བྱ་ནང་གི་སྒྱག་པ་ལ་བཀྱུ་མི་གིས་ནེས་ཀྱིས་ཞེས་ར་མ་ཕག་དུ་ཀྱུད་དུ་ཚལ་བ་བདང་བ་ལས། ར་ང་པོ་མ་ཕིན་པར་
རྒྱལ་བྲུ་གཉིས་ནེ་འོངས་ཀྱི། བྱ་ནང་གི་སྒྱག་པ་མ་ཉིས་སམ་ཀ་ར་ཉེས་ནྲ་ན། པོ་བོ་གཉིས་སྐྱད་ཀྱིས་བཏང་ན་ཏེ།
རེང་ཉིག་དུ་དཔྱགས་ཀྱང་མ་ཕྱིན་སྐྱུ་ཡང་མ་ནུས་ནས། དེའི་ཏོག་དུ་དཔྱགས་ཕྱིན་པ་དང་། སྒྲག་གིས་ཟོས་ས་
ཉེས་སྐྱུ་ས་སོ། །བྱ་མོ་ནེ་ར་སྐྱ་ར་སྐྱུ་ས་པ་ཕིས་ནས་ད་འམས་ཏེ། ས་ལ་འཁྱལ་ནས་རེ་ང་ཉིག་ཕིན་པ་དང་།
དཔྱགས་ཕྱི་ཏེ། སྒྱག་ཉིས་དང་བཅྱུན་མོ་དང་། པོ་བྲང་གི་སྐྱས་སུ་བཏས་ཏེ་ཕྱུར་པར་རྒྱལ་བྱ་ཀ་ང་དུ་ཆེ་འདྱོས་
པའི་གནས་སུ་སོང་ངོ་། །དེའི་ཚེ་སྒྱག་མོས་རྒྱལ་བྱའི་ཀ་ཉེ་ཟར་པར་ཟོས་ཞེན་ཀྱིས། ར་ས་པ་དང་ཁག་འཕའ་ཉིག་
གིས་ས་བཅྱོག་བཅྱོག་པ་ལྱུར་འདྲག་པ་མཐྱིང་ཏོ། །བཅྱུན་མོ་ནེ་མགོ་ནས་བརྒྱད་ཏོ། །རྒྱལ་པོས་ནེ་ལག་པ་ནས་
བརྒྱན་སྟེ། ཆེ་ཉིས་བདབ་ནས་དུ་ས་པ་དང་། དེ་ར་ཡང་དཔྱམས་ནས་ནེ་ར་ཉིག་ལྡིན་ཏེ། ཕྱེར་སངས་སོ། །རྒྱལ་
བྲུ་སེམས་ཅན་ཆེན་ཆེན་པོ་ནེ་དེ་ར་ཆེ་འདྱོས་ནས། དཀག་བ་འྱུག་ཕྱེའི་གནས་སུ་སྐྱེས་སོ། །ཏེ་ཆེའི་ཕྱེར་བདག་ཆེ་སྐྱུད་པས་
འདིར་སྐྱེས་སྐྱམ་བསམས་ཏེ། སྒྱེའི་མོག་གིས་ཀྱུན་དུ་བྱུ་ཀྱུད་དུ་བབྱས་ན། བདག་ཆེ་འགྲོས་པའི་དུས་ཕྱ་ཚལ་ན་
འདུག་པ་ལ་པ་མས་བསྒྱོར་ཏེ། ཀྱིན་དུ་ཡིད་ལ་གཅགས་པས། སྒྱ་ནང་ཏི་ཟྲག་རྩྲ་སྒྱག་བསྒྱལ་ནིང་ཆོ་ཉེས་
འདྲེལ་བ་མཐྱིང་ནས། ལུས་པསམས་པ། བདག་གི་པ་མ་འདེ་ལྱུར་མི་དཀག་བའི་རྒྱན་ཀྱིས་ཀག་ཏེ་ན་ལྱུས་དང་སྒྱག

གི་བར་རང་དུ་འགྱུར་གྱི། དེའི་སློབ་པ་བརྒྱུད་ཅིང་གནས་བྱར་འགྲོ་བའི་སྐྱམ་བསམས་ནས། ནམ་མཁའ་ལས་བབས་ཏེ་ སྐྱིང་གི་དམ་མཁན་ལས་ཆིག་སྲན་པ་དམ་པ་སྟུ་ཚོགས་ཀྱི་པ་ཁ་གཉིས་ལ་སློབ་བརྩི་དོ། །པ་མ་གཉིས་ཀྱི་ནམ་ མཁན་ལ་བབས་ནས། ལྔ་ཉིད་སུ་ཉེག་ལགས་པ་བདག་ལ་སློས་ཀིག་ཅེས་སྨས་པ་དང་། བདག་དེ་རྒྱལ་བུ་སེམས་ ཅན་ཆེན་པོ་ནེས་བྱ་བ་ཡིན་ཏེ། བདག་གིས་ལུས་ཀྱིས་སྟག་མོ་བྲོགས་པ་བསྲུད་བས་དཀའ་ལྲུང་གྱི་ལྲུའི་གནས་སུ་ སྐྱེས་སོ། །རྒྱལ་པོ་ཆེན་པོའི་བྱུར་མ་ཞིན་པར་མཛོད་ཅིག །ཅི་ཙམ་སྲེད་པ་དང་བཅས་པའི་ཆོས་ནི་མཐར་འཇིག་ ་པར་འོང་ངོ་། །སྐྱི་བ་ཡིད་དུ་དེས་པར་འཇིག་གོ །སྲོག་པ་ཐུག་ད་སེམས་ཅན་དཀྲལ་བར་ལྲུང་ངོ་། །དགེ་བ་ བྱས་ན་མཐོ་རིས་སུ་སྐྱེས་ཏེ། སྲུ་བ་དང་འཇིག་པ་ཀུལ་ལ་སྲིད་ན། ཅེའི་སྲུད་དུ་དཀའ་བ་འབར་ཞིག་གེ་ཕྱེར་རྒྱུ་ ངན་གྱི་རྒྱ་མཚོར་ལྲུང་བ་མི་ཚོར་རམ། དགེ་བའི་ཆོས་ལ་བརྩོན་འགྲུས་མཛོད་ཅེས་པ་དང་། དེའི་པ་མས་སྨྲས་པ། ཉིད་ནི་སྲིང་རྗེ་ཆེན་པོས་སྐུག་མོ་བསྲད་དེ་ཐབས་ཅད་ལ་སྲིང་བརྩེ་བ་ཡིན་ན། བདག་ཅག་བདག་སྟེ། ཆོའི་དུས་ བྱས་བས། དེ་ནི་ཉིད་དན་པའི་ཕྱིར་ཁ་ཡང་དུམ་བུ་དུམ་བུར་རད་པ་ཚམ་དུ་སྲུག་བསྲལ་གྱིས་གདུངས་ཏེ། སྟིང་ རྗེ་ཆེན་པོ་སྲྱིད་པ་ཞིན་འདི་ལྲུར་བྱ་བའི་རིགས་སམ། དེ་ནས་ཡང་ལྲུ་དེས་ཆིག་སྲུན་པ་ནམ་པ་སྲུ་ཚོགས་ཀྱི་སྒྲོ་་་་ ནས་བདམས་ཏེ། སློབ་བསྒྱུད་བས་དེའི་པ་མ་ཡང་སློབ་ཚུང་རད་སྲུས་ནས། རེན་པོ་ཆེ་སྲུ་བདུན་གྱི་སྐྱོམ་བྱས་ཏེ། དུས་བྱུ་དེའི་རང་དུ་བརྔག་སྟེ་སྲུས་པའི་སྟིང་དུ་མཆོད་རྟེན་བྱས་སོ། །ལྔ་ཡང་ཕྱིར་གནས་སུ་སོང་ངོ་། །རྒྱལ་པོ་ དང་འཁོར་མང་པོ་རྣམས་ཀྱང་ཕྱིར་པོ་གནང་དུ་སོང་ངོ་། །བཅོམ་ལྲུན་འདས་ཀྱིས་ཀུན་དགའ་པོ་ལ་བཀའ་སྩལ་པ། ཉིད་ཀྱི་ཡིད་ལ་ཅི་སྣམ་དུ་སེམས། དེའི་ཚེ་དེའི་དུས་ན་རྒྱལ་པོ་གིང་ཏ་ཆེན་པོ་སུ་ཡིན་སྲམ་སེམས། དེ་ནི་དལྟར་ བའི་ཡབ་རྒྱལ་པོ་ཟས་གཙང་མ་ཡིན་ནོ། །དེའི་ཚེ་དེའི་དུས་རྒྱལ་པོ་དེའི་བཙུན་མོ་དེ་ནི་དལྟར་འདི་ཡུམ་སྐྱ་མ་ལྔ་ མཛེས་ཡིན་ནོ། །དེའི་དུས་ན་སྲས་ར་བ་སྒྲ་ཆེན་པོ་དེ་ནི་ཕྲམས་པ་ཡིན་ནོ། །སྲས་འབྲིང་པོ་ནི་བ་མི་སུ་ད་ཡིན་ནོ། ། དེའི་ཚེ་དེའི་དུས་ན་རྒྱལ་བུ་ཐ་ཆུང་སེམས་ཅན་ཆེན་པོ་དེ་དེ་གདན་དུ་མ་སེམས་ཤིག །ད་ལྟར་ང་ཡིན་ནོ། །དེའི་ ཚེ་དེའི་དུས་ན། སྟག་ཕྲག་ཏེ་མི་འདི་གཉིས་ཡིན་ཏེ། ནས་སྟོན་ཡང་ཡུད་ཏེ་ང་པོ་ནས་བགེགས་ལས་ཐར་བར་བྱུ་ ཏེ་སྟོག་སྒྲུབས་ནས་བདེ་བར་བྱས་སོ། །ད་མཆོད་པར་རངས་རྒྱལ་དན་ནས་ཀྱང་བགེགས་ལས་ཐར་བར་མཛོད་ནས། འབྱེར་ བའི་སྲུག་བསྲལ་ཆེན་པོ་ལས་ཡིངས་སུ་བྲོལ་ལོ། །དེའི་ཚེ་ད་ཀྱུ་དགའ་པོ་དང་། འབྱེར་མང་པོ་ཐབྲ་རང་བཆར་ ལྲུད་འདས་ཀྱིས་གསུངས་པ་ལ་མཆོན་པར་བསྲད་དོ། །   །སེམས་ཅན་ཆེན་པོས་སྟག་མོ་ལ་ལྲུས་ཀྱིན་པའི་ལེ་དུ་སྟེ་ གཉིས་པའོ། །

VOCABULARY

This vocabulary contains all the words found in the reading exercises on pages 84–85 and 92–102.

It is arranged alphabetically in Tibetan order (see p. 1). The arrangement of the vowels is a, i, u, e, o. Subjoined consonants (p. 7) follow the simple ones, e. g., bya after bo; superadded consonants (p. 8) are not counted, and such words are to be looked for under the original consonant, e. g., rta under ta, after ta, gta, etc.

Abbreviations: *pf.* = perfect root; *ipl.* = imperative root; *fut.* = future root; *n.* = noun; *pron.* = pronoun; *a.* = adjective; *adv* = adverb; *v.* = verb; *prep.* = preposition; *cj.* = conjunction; *n. p.* = proper noun.

ཀ

ཀུན་ *a.* whole; all

ཀུན་དགའ་བོ་ *n. p.* Ananda

ཀུན་དགའ་ར་བ་ *n.* grove

དཀའ་བ་ *n.* difficulty

བཀའ་ *n.* speech; order

བཀའ་དྲིན་ *n.* favor

བཀའ་སྩལ་བ་ *pf.*
    བསྩལ་ *v.* say

བཀྲ་མི་ཤིས་ *n.* calamity

བཀྲེས་པ་ *v.* be hungry

ཀང་པ་ *n.* foot; leg

ཀུ་བ་ *pf.* བཀུ་ *v.* steal

ཀྱེན་གྱིས་ *prep.* because of

སྐད་ *n.* speech voice

སྐོར་བ་ *pf.* བསྐོར་ *v.* surround

སྐྱབས་ *n.* help

སྐྱེ་བ་ *pf.* སྐྱེས་ *v.* be born

སྐྱེད་པ་ *pf.* བསྐྱེད་ *v.* cause

སྐྱོབ་པ་ *pf.* སྐྱབས་ *v.* save

སྐྲ་ *n.* hair of head

སྐྲག་དངང་བ་ *v.* be afraid

སྐོམ་པ་ *v.* be thirsty

བསྐལ་བ་ *n.* kalpa (aeon)

ཁ

ཁ་ *n.* mouth; face

ཁ་ན་ *adv.* above

ཁམས་ *n.* state of health

ཁྱིམ་ *n.* house

ཁོ་ *n.* husband

ཁྲ་ *n.* hawk

ཁྲག་ *n.* blood

ཁྲིམས་ *n.* law; justice

མཁས་པ་ *a.* wise

མཐེན་པ་ *v.* know; understand

འཁམས་པ་ *v.* swoon

འཁུར་བ་ *pf.* བཀུར་ *v.* carry

འཁོར་ *n.* retinue

འཁོར་བ་ *v.* turn

འཁོར་བ་ *n.* samskāra (circle of rebirths)

འཐེར་བ་ *pf.* ཁྱེར་ *v.* carry; bring

འཐིད་པ་ *pf.* ཁྱིད་ *v.* lead

ག

ག་རེ་ *adv.* where

གང་ *pron.* who, which

གང་ན་ *adv.* where

གང་སུ་ཡང་ *pron.* whoever

གལ་ཏེན་ *cj.* if

གོས་ *n.* dress

གྱངས་ *n.* number

གྱངས་མེད་པ་ *a.* innumerable

གྲོང་ཁྱེར་ *n.* town

དགའ་བ་ *v.* rejoice, *n.* joy

དགའ་ལྡན་ *n.* Tushita (heaven)

དགེ་བ་ *n.* virtue

དགོངས་པ་ *v.* think

དགྲ་ *n.* enemy

དགྲ་བཅོམ་པ་ *n.* Arhat

བགེགས་ *n.* obstacle

བགོ་བ་ *n.* clothes

བགོ་བ་ *pf.* བགོས་ *v.* wear

བགྱིད་པ་ *pf.* བགྱི་ *v.* do; make

མགོ་(བོ་) *n.* head

མགོན་མེད་ཟས་སྦྱིན་ *n. p.* Anathapindada

འགར་ *a.* several

འགུམ་པ་ *v.* die

འགྱེལ་བ་ *v.* fall

འགྲེ་བ་ *v.* roll

འགྲོ་བ་ *pf.* སོང་ *v.* go

འགྲོགས་ཏེ་ *adv.* together

འགྲོལ་བ་ *pf.* གྲོལ་ *v.* become
  free

རྒན་མོ་ *n.* old woman

རྒལ་བ་ *pf.* བརྒལ་ *v.* climb

གོད་མ་ *n.* mare

རྒྱ་མཚོ་ *n.* ocean

རྒྱང་ནས་ *adv.* from afar

རྒྱང་མ་ *n.* distance

རྒྱལ་པོ་ *n.* king

རྒྱལ་ཕྲན་ *n.* vassal

རྒྱལ་བ་ *v.* win

རྒྱལ་བྱེད་ *n. p.*

རྒྱུད་ *n.* string; tantra

རྒྱུད་ལྔ་ *n.* the 5 natures

སྒྲོ་བ་ *pf.* བསྒྲོ་ *v.* say; bid

སྒྱུ་མ་ *n. p.* Māyā

སྒྲ་ *n.* sound; voice; word

སྒྲ་ཅན་པོ་ *n. p.*

སྒྲོག་པ་ *v.* tie; bind

སྒྲོམ་ *n.* box; coffin

བརྒྱལ་བ་ *v.* swoon

བསྒོ་བ་ *pf.* བསྒོས་ *v.* soil

ང

ངལ་བ་ *v.* be tired

ངུ་བ་ *v.* weep *pf.* ངུས་

དྭངས་སྐྱིག་ *a.* orange (color)

ངེས་ཀྱིས་ *adv.* evidently

ངེས་པར་ *adv.* certainly

ངོ་མཚར་ཆེ་བ་ *n.* miracle

དངོས་པོ་ *n.* matter; event

མནའ་བ་ *v.* be

མཐོན་པར་ *adv.* clearly

སྤུག་པ་ *pf.* སྤུགས་ *v.* praise

སྔར་ *adv.* ahead; before

སྔོན་ *adv.* formerly

སྔོན་འདས་པ་ *a.* previous

ཙ

ཅན་ *a.* equipped with

ཅེ་ *pron.* what

ཅི་ལྟར་ *adv.* how

ཅི་ཙམ་ *a.* how much

ཅེའི་ཕྱིར་ *adv.* why

ཅི་རིགས་པ་ *adv.* in part

ཅུང་ཟད་ *adv.* a little

ཅེས་ *adv.* thus (direct
     quotation)

གཅགས་པ་ *v.* understand

གཅོག་པ་ *pf.* བཅག་ *v.* break

གཅོད་པ་ *pf.* བཅད་ *v.* cut;
     decide

བཅས་ཏེ་ *adv.* together

བཅས་པ་ *a.* connected

བཅུག་ see འཇུག་

བཅོམ་ལྡན་འདས་ *a.* victorious

ལྗེ་ *n.* tongue

ཆ

ཆད་པ་ *n.* punishment

ཆུ་བོ་ *n.* river

ཆུང་ *a.* small; young

ཆུང་དུ་ནས་ from infancy

ཆུང་མ་ *n.* wife

ཆུང་ཟད་ *a.* a little

ཆུད་གསན་པ་ *v.* waste

ཆེན་པོ་ *a.* great

ཆོ་ང་ *n.* lament

ཆོད་པ་ *v.* cut off

ཆོས་ *n.* religion; matter

ཆོས་གོས་ *n.* clerical dress

མཆི་བ་ *v.* come; go

མཆེད་ *n.* brother

མཆོངས་པ་ *v.* jump

མཆོད་རྟེན་ *n.* stupa, shrine

འཆག་པ་ *v.* walk

ཇ

ཇི་ what (see ཅི་)

འཇིག་པ་ *pf.* བཞིག་ *v.* perish

འཇིགས་པ་ *v.* fear

འཇུག་པ་ *pf.* བཅུག་ *v.* insert

འཇུག་པ་ *pf.* ཞུགས་ *v.* enter; walk;

ཇེ་ *n.* lord

ཇེས་ *n.* footprint

ཇོད་པ་ *pf.* བཇོད་ *v.* speak

ཉ

ཉམ་ཆུང་ *a.* sad; faint

ཉལ་བ་ *v.* lie down

ཉིད་ *n.* self

ཉིན་པར་ at daytime

ཉེད་པ་ *v.* be pressed

ཉེས་པ་ *v.* be hurt

ཉེས་པ་ *n.* crime; sin

གཉེར་བ་ *v.* look after

མཉན་ *n. p.* Shrāvastī

རྙེད་པ་ *v.* get

སྙད་པ་ *pf.* བསྙད་ *v.* report

སྙམ་ *n.* mind

སྙམ་པ་ *v.* think

སྙིང་ *n.* heart

སྙིང་བརྩེ་བ་ *v.* love; pity

སྙིང་རྗེ་ *n.* mercy

སྙེད་ *adv.* about

སྙོད་པ་ *pf.* བསྙོད་ *v.* feed

བཅུ་བ་ *pf.* བཅུས་ *v.* borrow

ཏ

གཏམ་ *n.* speech

གཏད་ *adv.* like, as

གཏད་ *n.* news; rumor

ལྟུང་བ་ *pf.* ལྟུང་ *v.* fall

གཏི་མུག་ *n.* ignorance

ལྟོགས་པ་ *v.* be hungry

གཏིང་ *n.* bottom

སྟག་ཕྲུག་ *n.* tiger cub

གཏིང་ཟབ་པོ་ *a.* deep

སྟག་མོ་ *n.* tigress

གཏོང་བ་ *pf.* བཏང་ *v.* give;
    let (go)

སྟན་པ་ *a.* kind; sweet

རྟ་ *n.* horse

སྟེང་ནས་ *adv.* off, down

རྟག་ཏུ་ *adv.* always

སྟོབས་ *n.* strength

རྟོག་པ་ *pf.* བརྟག་ *v.* search;
    consider

སྟེའུ་ *n.* axe

ལྟ་བ་ *pf.* བལྟས་ *v.* look

སྟོད་པ་ *pf.* བསྟོད་ *v.* praise

ལྟ་བུ་ *adv.* like, as

སྟོན་པ་ *pf.* བསྟན་ *v.* show

སྟོར་བ་ *v.* be lost; stray

ཕ

ཕ་ག་པ་ *n.* weaver

ཕ་ཅུང་ *a.* last (of three)

ཕགས་ *n.* fabric

ཕ་དུ་ *adv.* towards

ཕམས་ཅད་ *a.* whole

ཕར་བ་ *v.* become free

ཕལ་མོ་ *n.* palm of hand

ཕལ་མོ་སྦྲང་བ་ fold hands

ཕུག་པ་ *v.* arrive

ཕུགས་ *n.* mind; heart

ཕུགས་རྗེ་ཆེན་པོ་ *n. p.* Avalo-
kiteshvara

ཕབ་པ་ *v.* overcome; be able

ཕྲོགས་པ་ *v.* strike; stumble;
hold

ཕྲོབ་པ་ *v.* get; find

ཕྲོས་པ་ *v.* hear

མཕར་ *adv.* finally; altogether

མཕུ་ *n.* force

མཕྲོ་རིས་ *n.* paradise

མཕྲོང་བ་ *v.* see

འཕགས་པ་ *pf.* བཕགས་
v. weave

ད

ད་ལྟར་ *adv.* now

དང་བཅས་ *prep.* together
with

དང་བ་ *a.* pure; pious

དུམ་ *a.* many

དུམ་བུ་ *n.* fragment

དུས་ *n.* time

དེ་ཅིའི་ཕྱིར་ *adv.* why

དེ་ཉིད་ *pron.* the same

དེ་སྙེད་ *a.* how many

དེ་བཞིག་གཤེགས་པ་ *n. p.* Tathāgata

དེ་ཡང་ *adv.* thus

དེར་ *adv.* then

དོགས་པ་ *v.* fear

དོན་ *n.* idea; affair; boon

དྲག་ཏུ་ *adv.* strongly

དྲག་པ་ *a.* strong

དྲང་པོ་ *a.* straight

དྲན་པ་ *v.* remember

དྲལ་གྱིས་ *adv.* gently

དྲལ་བ་ *a.* gentle

དྲེམ་ *a.* dirty

དྲིན་ *n.* kindness

དྲིན་དྲན་པ་ *v.* be grateful

དྲུང་དུ་ *adv.* near; before

དྲོན་མོ་ *a.* warm

གདུངས་པ་ *v.* be afflicted

གདོན་མོ་ཙ་བར་ *adv.* certainly

བདག་པོ་ *n.* master

བདེ་བ་ *n.* bliss *v.* be happy

བདེན་པ་ *v.* be true

མདུན་ *adv.* previously

འདར་བ་ *pf.* འདས་ *v.* overcome

འདི་ལྟ་བུ་ one like him

འདིར་ *adv.* here

འདུག་པ་ *v.* sit; dwell; be

འདེབས་པ་ *pf.* བཏབ་ *v.* cast; do

འདོང་བ་ *pf.* དོང་ *v.* go

འདོད་ཆགས་ *n.* lust

འདྲ་བ་ *a.* similar

འདྲི་བ་ *pf.* དྲིས་ *v.* ask

འདྲེན་པ་ *pf.* དྲངས་ *v.* pull

རྡབ་པ་ *pf.* བརྡབས་ *v.* throw down

རྡུལ་ *n.* dust

རྡོ་ *n.* stone

ལྡག་པ་ *pf.* བལྡག་ *v.* lick

ལྡན་པ་ *pf.* ལྡས་ *v.* rise; suffice

ཕྱོག་པ་ *pf.* ལྡོག་ *v.* return

ཕྱིག་པ་ *v.* sin

སྡུག་བསྔལ་ *n.* suffering

སྡུག་བསྔལ་བ་ *v.* suffer

སྡུག་པ་ *a.* beloved

ན

ནང་ན་ *adv.* inside

ནམ་མཁའ་ *n.* sky; heaven

ནུ་བོ་ *n.* younger brother

ནུས་པ་ *v.* be able

ནོར་བདག་ *n.* rich man

གནང་བ་ *v.* give; allow

གནས་ *n.* place

མནལ་ *n.* sleep; dream

རྡང་བ་ *pf.* བརྡངས་ *v.* choke

རྣམ་པ་ *n.* manner

རྣོན་པོ་ *a.* sharp

སྣ་ *n.* kind; sort

སྣ་ཚོགས་ *a.* various

སྣད་པ་ *pf.* བསྣད་ *v.* hurt

སྣོམ་པ་ *pf.* བསྣོམས་ *v.* take

པ

སྤུ་ *n.* hair

སྤྱི་བོ་ *n.* crown of head

སྤྱི་བོས་ཕྱག་འཚལ་བ་ *v.* bow down

སྤྱོད་པ་ *pf.* སྤྱད་ *v.* do; use | སྤྲོ་བ་ *n.* joy

པ

པ་མ་ *n.* parents

པ་རོལ་ *adv.* beyond; ago

པག་ *a.* hidden

པན་པ་ *v.* be useful

ཕུག་རོན་ *n.* pigeon

ཕོ་བོ་ *n.* elder brother

ཕོ་བྲང་ *n.* house; palace

ཕྱག་ཚལ་བ་ *v.* greet

ཕྱི་རོལ་ *adv.* outside

ཕྱིན་པ་ *v.* arrive

ཕྱིར་ *adv.* again; by; for

ཕྱིར་སང་བ་ *pf.* སངས་ *v.* recover

ཕུང་ *see* འཕྱིན་པ་

ཕྱིས་ *see* འཕྱིད་པ་

ཕྱོགས་ *n.* side

ཕྲག་པ་ *n.* shoulder

འཕུར་བ་ *pf.* ཕུར་ *v.* fly

འཕོ་བ་ *pf.* འཕོས་ *v.* die

འཕོག་པ་ *pf.* ཕོག་ *v.* hit; touch

འཕྱད་པ་ *pf.* ཕྱད་ *v.* meet

འཕྲོག་པ་ *pf.* ཕྲོགས་ *v.* steal

བ

བ་གླང་ *n.* bull

བར་ *adv.* between

བར་ཆད་ *n.* risk

བར་འགར་ *adv.* sometimes

བུ་ *n.* son

བུ་པོ་ *n.* son

བུར་མེད་ *n.* woman

བྱམས་པ་ *n.* kindness

བྱམས་པ་ *n. p.* Maitreya

བྱའི་བར་དུ་ *adv.* meanwhile

བྱེད་པ་ *pf.* བྱས་ *fut.* བྱ་ *v.* do; make

བྲམ་ཟེ་ *n.* brahmin

བླ་ *adv.* above; superior

བླ་ *n.* soul

བློ་ *n.* intellect

བློན་པོ་ *n.* minister

དབང་ *n.* power

དབང་བྱེད་པ་ *v.* rule

དབུགས་ *n.* breath

དབུལ་འཕོངས་ *a.* poor

དབྱུག་པ་ *n.* stick

འབའ་ཞིག་ *adv.* only

འབབ་པ་ *pf.* བབས་ *v.* descend

འབོར་བ་ *pf.* བོར་ *v.* fasten

འབྲི་བ་ *pf.* བྲི་ *v.* fall off

འབྱིན་བ་ *pf.* བྱུང་ *v.* produce, send out

འབྱུང་བ་ *pf.* བྱུང་ *v.* become

འབྱེད་པ་ *pf.* ཕྱེས་ *v.* open

འབྲིང་པོ་ *a.* middle (of three)

སྦེད་པ་ *pf.* སྦས་ *v.* hide

སྦྱིན་པ་ *pf.* བྱིན་ *v.* give back

སྦྱོར་བ་ *pf.* སྦྱར་ *v.* conform

མ

མ་ *n.* mother

མ་ཐག་དུ་ *cj.* as soon as

མ་ཐག་པ་ *adv.* just now

མ་སྲུད་ *n.* mother and children

མ་ཟད་ཀྱི་ *adv.* not only

མང་པོ་ *a.* numerous

མི་ *n.* man

མི་ཉམས་པ་ *a.* perfect

མིག་ *n.* eye

མུ་གེ་ *n.* misery

མྱུར་དུ་ *adv.* quickly

མྱུར་བར་ *adv.* quickly

མྱི་ལམ་ *n.* dream

མྱི་བ་ *pf.* མྱིས་ *v.* dream

སྨྲར་བ་ *pf.* སྨྲས་ *v.* say

སྨྲ་བ་ *see* སྨྲར་བ་

ཙ

ཙམ་དུ་ *cj.* so that

ཙམ་ཞིག་ *adv.* as much as

གཙོ་བོ་ *a.* excellent

བཙུན་མོ་ *n.* lady; queen

བཙོག་པ་ *a.* unclean

ཙིག་པ་ *n.* wall

ཉིགས་པ་ *v.* build

ཉེ་བ་ *v.* play; frolic

ཙོག་ཙོག་ *adv.* squatting

ཙོད་པ་ *pf.* བཙད་ *v.* quarrel

བཅེ་བ་ *v.* love

བཙོན་འགྲུས་མཛད་པ་ *v.* use diligence

ཚ

ཚང་ *n.* lair; nest

ཚལ་ *n.* garden; grove

ཚལ་བ་ *n.* splinter

ཚིག་ *n.* word

ཚིག་སྙན་པ་ *n.* kind words

ཚུར་ཤོག *int.* come here!

ཚེ་ *n.* time; life

ཚོར་བ་ *v.* perceive

འཚོལ་བ་ *pf.* བཙོལ་ *v.* seek

ཇ

མཛད་པ་ *ipt.* མཛོད་ *v.* do; perform

མཛེས་པ་ *a.* beautiful

འཛད་པ་ *pf.* ཟད་ *v.* be spent

འཛམ་བུ་གླིང་ *n.p.* Jambud-vipa(=India)

འཛིན་པ་ *pf.* བཟུང་ *v.* seize

ཇ་ *n.* clay; pot

ཞ

ཞག་ *n.* day

ཞབས་ *n.* foot

ཞལ་ཆེ་ *n.* judgment

ཞལ་ཆེ་བ་ *n.* judge

ཞིང་ *n.* field

ཞེ་སྡང་ *n.* hatred

ཞེས་ *see* ཅེས་

གཞན་ *a.* other

བཞམས་པ་ *v.* caress; pacify

བཞིག *see* འཇིག་པ་

བཞིན་དུ་ *adv.* according to

བཞུགས་པ་ *v.* sit; dwell

ཟ

ཟ་བ་ *pf.* བཟས་ or ཟོས་ *v.* eat

ཟན་ *n.* food

ཟབ་པོ་ *a.* deep

ཟས་ *n.* food

ཟས་གཙང་མ་ *n. p.* Shuddhodana

ཟིན་པ་ *see* འཛིན་པ་

ཟིན་པ་ *v.* finish

ཟུག་རྡུ་ *n.* pain

ཟེར་བ་ *v.* say

གཟིར་བ་ *v.* be afflicted

བཟའ་བ་ *n.* food

ཡ

ཡབ་ *n.* father

ཡིད་ *n.* soul; mind

ཡིད་ཚིམ་པ་ *v.* satisfy

ཡུན་ *n.* time

ཡུམ་ *n.* mother

ཡུལ་ *n.* place

ཡོངས་སུ་ *adv.* completely

ཡོན་ཏན་ *n.* virtue

ར

ར་བ་ *n.* fence; wall

རང་ *adv.* by itself

རབ་ *a.* first (of three)

རབ་ཏུ་ *adv.* very

རབ་བྱུང་ *n.* cleric

རིགས་ངན་ *n.* hangman

རིགས་པ་ *a.* proper

རིང་པོ་ *a.* long; far

རིང་ཞིག་ཏུ་ *adv.* for a long time

རིད་པ་ *a.* emaciated

རིན་པོ་ཆེ་ *a.* precious; *n.* jewel

རུང་བ་ *v.* be; be fit

རུས་པ་ *n.* bone

རུས་བུ་ *n.* bones

རེ་ *a.* single; each

ལ

ལག་པ་ *n.* hand; arm

ལགས་པ་ *v.* be

ལང་བ་ *pf.* ལངས་ *v.* rise

ལན་ *n.* times; turns

ལམ་ *n.* way; road

ལུས་ *n.* body

ལུས་པ་ *v.* remain

ལེགས་པ་ *a.* good; happy

ལེའུ་ *n.* chapter

ལོན་པ་ *v.* elapse

ཤ

ཤ་ *n.* flesh

ཤ་རྫོན་ *n.* raw meat

ཤམ་ཐབས་ *n.* robe

ཤི་བ་ *v.* die

ཤིང་ *n.* wood

ཤིང་རྟ་ *n.* carriage

ཤིང་རྟ་ཆེན་པོ་ *n. p.* Mahā-ratha

ཤིན་ཏུ་ *adv.* very

ཤེས་ *see* ཅེས་

གཤེགས་པ་ *v.* go; come

ས

ས་ *n.* earth; ground

སངས་རྒྱས་ *n. p.* Buddha

སད་པ་ *v.* awake

སུ་ཞིག་ *pron.* who; which

སེམ་པ་ *pf.* བསམས་ *v.* think

སེམས་ *n.* soul; mind

སེམས་ཅན་ཆེན་པོ་ *n. p.*

སེམས་ཅན་དམྱལ་བ་ *n.* hell

སོ་ *n.* tooth

སྲས་ *n.* son

སྲིད་པ་ *v.* fall to the lot

སྲེད་པ་ *n.* desire

སྲོག་ *n.* life

སྤྱད་དུ་ *adv.* for the sake

སྤྱད་བཞིན་པར་ *adv.* behind

སྦས་ *n.* retinue

གསན་པ་ *v.* listen

གསུང་བ་ *pf.* གསུངས་ *v.* say

གསོ་བ་ *pf.* བསོས་ *v.* feed; rear

གསོད་པ་ *pf.* བསད་ *v.* kill

གསོལ་བ་ *v.* say; ask

གསོལ་བ་འདེབས་པ་ *v.* make a request

བསོད་སྙོམས་ *n.* alms

བསོད་ནམས་ *n.* good deed

ཧ

ལྷ་ *n.* god; king

ལྷ་མོ་ *n.* goddess; queen

ལྷག་མ་ *n.* remainder

ལྷུང་ *see* ལྷུང་བ་

ལྷུང་བཟེད་ *n.* alms bowl

A list of the more frequent verbs *).

a) Four-rooted verbs.

Pres.	Perf.	Fut.	Imperv.		WT
འགེགས་པ་	བཀག་	དགག་	ཁོག་	stop, hinder.	kag-če
འགེངས་པ་	བཀང་	དགང་	ཁོང་	fill.	kaṅ-če
འགེལ་བ་	བཀལ་	དགལ་	ཁོལ་	lade, put on . . .	kal-če
གཅོད་པ་	བཅད་	གཅད་	ཆོད་	cut.	čad-če imprv. čod
འཆིང་བ་	བཅིངས་	བཅིང་	ཆིང་	tie, bind.	
འཆོ་བ་ འཆོས་པ་	བཅོ(ས)་	བཅོ་	ཆོས་	make.	čo-če pf. and imp. čos
འཇིག་པ་	(བ)ཞིག་	གཞིག་	ཞིགས་	destroy.	šig-če
འཇུག་པ་	བཅུག་	གཞུག་	ཆུག་	put in.	čug-če
འཇོག་པ་	བཞག་	གཞག་	ཞོག་	put, place. (C: žag-pá)	
འཇོག་པ་	བཞོགས་	གཞོག་	ཞོག་	cut.	žog-če
གཏོང་བ་	བཏང་	གཏང་	ཐོང་	give.	taṅ-če imp. toṅ
ལྟ་བ་	བལྟས་	བལྟ་	ལྟོས་	look.	(l)ta-če

---

*) They are here arranged according to the number of the roots, though these are in many instances, not so strictly observed, even in printed books, as they ought to be. It should especially be remarked that the mute ས་ in the perf. and imp. is in most cases either put or omitted very arbitrarily.

Pres.	Perf.	Fut.	Imperv.		WT
འདེགས་པ་	བདེག་	གདེགས་	ཐེག་	lift; weigh. imp.	*tag-če* *tog*
འདེབས་པ་	བདབ་	གདབ་	ཐོབ་	throw. imp.	*tab-če* *tob*
འདོགས་པ་	བདགས་	གདགས་	ཐོགས་	tie, bind. imp.	*tag-če* *tog,* *tag toṅ*
འདོན་པ་	བཏོན་	གཏོན་	ཐོན་	get, drive, out. always for འབྱིན་པ་	*ton-če*
འཕེན་པ་	འཕངས་	འཕང་	ཕོང་	throw, hurt.	*p̔aṅ-če*
བྱེད་པ་	བྱས་	བྱ་	བྱོས་	do, make. for it	*čo-če*
འབེབས་པ་	ཕབ་	དབབ་	ཕོབ་	bring, let, down.	*p̔ab-če*
འཚག་པ་	{འཚགས་ / བཙགས་}	བཙག་	ཚོག་	filter, sift.	*ts̔ag-če*
འཚོང་བ་	བཙོངས་	བཙོང་	ཚོང་	sell.	*tsoṅ-če*
འཛིན་པ་	གཟུང་, ཟིན་	གཟུང་	ཟུང་	seize.	*zum-če*
ལེན་པ་	བླངས་	བླང་	ལོང་(ས་), ལོན་	take.	*len-če, laṅ-če*
སློབ་པ་	བསླབ་(ས་)་	བསླབ་	སློབ་	learn; teach.	*lab-če*

---

b) Three-rooted verbs.

Pres.	Perf.	Fut.	Imperv.		WT
འཁུར་བ་	བཀུར་		ཁུར་	carry.	*k̔ur-če*
འཁྱོང་བ་	ཁྱངས་		ཁྱོང་	bring. for འཁྱེར་བ་	*k̔yoṅ-če*

Pres.	Perf.	Fut.	Imperv.		WT
རྒྱབ་པ་	བརྒྱབ་		རྒྱོབ་	throw, cast.	gyab-če
					imp. gyob
					for འདེབས་པ་
རྒྱུག་པ་	(བ)རྒྱུག(ས)་		རྒྱུག་	run.	gyug-če
གཅོག་པ་	བཅག་		ཆོག་	break.	čag-če,
					imp. čog
འཆད་པ་	བཤད་		ཤོད་	tell, explain.	śad-če
རྟེན་པ་	བརྟེན་		རྟོན་	hold.	ten-če
འདྲེན་པ་	དྲང་		དྲོངས་	draw.	to lead: ran-če
					to remove: den̄-če
འབབ་པ་	བབ(ས)་		ཕོབ(ས)་	descend.	
འབུད་པ་	ཕུ(ས)་	དབུ་	ཕུས་	blow (act.).	p̓u-če
འབུད་པ་	ཕུད་	དབུད་	ཕུད་	put off, drop (act.).	p̓ud-če
འབྱིན་པ་	ཕྱུང་	དབྱུང་	ཕྱུང་	take, pull, out.	p̓in-če
འབྱེད་པ་	ཕྱེ(ས)་	དབྱེ་	ཕྱེ(ས)་	open (act.).	p̓e-če,
					imp. p̓e(s).
སྨྲ་བ་	སྨྲས་		སྨྲོས་	say.	s. ཟེར་བ་
ལང་བ་	ལངས་		ལོང་	rise.	lan̄-če

---

c) Two-rooted verbs.

Pres.	Perf.	Imperv.		WT
སྐྱེ་བ་	སྐྱེས་		be born.	skye-ce
སྐྱེད་པ་	བསྐྱེད་		bear, beget.	skye-če
འཁྱེར་བ་	ཁྱེར་	ཁྱེར་	carry.	k̓yer-če

Pres.	Perf.	Imperv.		WT
འགྱུར་བ་	གྱུར་	གྱུར་	become.	*gyur-če*
འགྲོ་བ་	སོང་	སོང་	go; become.	*do-če*
			[only in certain sentences.	
སྒྱུར་བ་	བསྒྱུར་	སྒྱུར་	alter.	*gyur-če*
ངུ་བ་	ངུས་		weep.	*ṅu-če*
འཆི་བ་	ཤི་		die.	*ši-če*
འཆོར་བ་	ཤོར་		flee.	*šor-če*
འཛུག་པ་	ཞུགས་	ཞུགས་	enter.	*žug-če*
ཉི་བ་	ཉོས་		buy.	*ño-če*
སྡོད་པ་	བསྡད་	སྡོད་	sit; stay.	*dad-če*
				imp. *dod*
འཕེལ་བ་	ཕེལ་		increase (neutr.).	*p̌el-če*
བླུག་པ་	བླུག(ས)་	བླུག(ས)་	pour.	*lug-če*
འབུད་པ་	བུད་		blow (neutr.).	*p̌u-če*
འབོད་པ་	བོས་	བོས་	call.	*bo-če,*
				imp. *bos (boi, bǒ).*
འབྱུང་བ་	བྱུང་		appear, originate.	*juṅ-če*
སྤྱོང་བ་	སྤྱང་		enjoy.	*ñaṅ-če*
རྩིག་པ་	བརྩིགས་	བརྩིགས་	build up.	*tsig-če*
ཞུ་བ་	ཞུས་	ཞུས་	ask.	*žu-če*
				(ju-če)
སླེབ་པ་	བསླེབས་		arrive.	*leb-če*

d) One-rooted verb.

WT

དགའ་བ་	be glad, to like.	Ld. *ɣa-če*, W besides འཕྲད་པ་
འགྱེལ་བ་	fall, drop.	*ḍil-če*, also འཛིལ་(བ་)
མཆོང་བ་, མཆོངས་པ་	leap, jump.	*čoṅ-če*
ཉལ་བ་	lie down.	*ñal-če*
ཐུག་པ་	meet.	*t̆ug-če*
ཐུབ་པ་	be able.	*t̆ub-če*
ཐོབ་པ་	find, get.	*tob-če*
ཐོས་པ་	hear.	(*t̆sor-če*)
མཐོང་བ་	see.	*t̆oṅ-če*
འཕྲད་པ་	be glad, to like.	*t̆ad-če*, nearly always for དགའ་བ་ and འདོད་པ་
འཕྲོན་པ་	come out, go out.	*t̆on-če*, usual for འབྱུང་བ་
འདོད་པ་	wish, like, desire.	rare.
ནུས་པ་	be able.	s. ཐུབ་པ་
གནས་པ་	stay, dwell, remain.	*nas* (*nai*, *nạ̈*) - *če*, but usually: *dad-če*
འབར་བ་	burn.	*bar-če*
ཚོར་བ་	perceive.	*t̆sor-če*, and usual for ཐོས་པ་
མཛད་པ་	do, make (resp.)	*dzad-če*, imp. *dzod*.

		WT
ཟེར་བ་	say.	*zer-če*, usual for སྨྲ་བ་
ལུས་པ་	remain, be left.	*lus-če*
ལོག་པ་	turn back, return.	*log-če*
ཤེས་པ་	know.	*šes (šē)-če*
(ཧ་)གོ་བ་	understand.	*há-go-če*

———— ◆◆ ————

DATE DUE